KU-470-852

Impact Assignments in English

Second Edition

by R. B. Heath

Head of the Department of English
Wellesbourne School,
High Wycombe

Longman

LONGMAN GROUP LIMITED
London
*Associated companies, branches and representatives
throughout the world*

This edition © Longman Group Ltd 1968, 1975
*All rights reserved. No part of this publication may be
reproduced, stored in a retrieval system or transmitted in any
form or by any means, electronic, mechanical, photocopying,
recording or otherwise, without the prior permission of the
copyright owner*

First published 1968
Twelfth impression 1974
Second edition 1975
Fifth impression 1980

ISBN 0 582 21658 3

Printed in Hong Kong by
Sheck Wah Tong Printing Press Ltd

Acknowledgements.

We are grateful to the following for permission to reproduce copyright material: Aldus Books Ltd for an extract from *Man and Insects* by L. Hugh Newman; author's agents for an extract from Act IV of *Becket* by Jean Anouilh; the author for 'Marsh Marigolds' by Gene Baro; Ernest Benn Ltd for an extract from *History Unearthed* by Sir Leonard Woolley; The Bodley Head Ltd for 'Chough' from *Poems and Contradictions* by Rex Warner; Chatto and Windus Ltd for an extract from *Maidens' Trip* by Emma Smith; The Clarendon Press for extracts from the *Oxford Junior Encyclopaedia* Vol. III; The Cotton Board for an extract from *Introducing Cotton*; author's representatives and Sidgwick and Jackson Ltd for an extract from *Abraham Lincoln* by John Drinkwater; *Encyclopaedia Britannica* (1964 printing) for the passage on 'Marijuana'; Faber and Faber Ltd for 'The Express' from *Collected Poems* by Stephen Spender and an **extract** from 'Summertime' by Ugo Betti from *Three Plays* translated by Henry Reed; the Executors of the Ernest Hemingway Estate and Jonathan Cape Ltd for 'The Clark's Fork Valley, Wyoming' by Ernest Hemingway; The Controller of Her Majesty's Stationery Office for figures from tables 27, 28, 29, 30 and 31 in *Statistics of Education* 1972 Vol. I, Schools which appeared in an article 'Special Teaching for Special Children' by Paul Medlicott in *New Society* 21st March, 1974 and an extract from *The Roman Forts of the Saxon Shore* by Leonard Cottrell; Holt, Rinehart and Winston, Inc. New York and Jonathan Cape Ltd for 'Out, Out...' from *Complete Poems of Robert Frost*, Copyright 1916 by Holt, Rimehart and Winston, Inc: Copyright 1944 by Robert Frost; author for *The Rain-Horse* by Ted Hughes; Independent Television Authority for extracts from *Parents, Children and Television;* Author for 'Young Gazelle' from *The Collected Poems of Babette Deutsch* published by Doubleday and Co. Inc; IPC Magazines Ltd for Tables illustrating a new measurement study of Women's Weekly Magazines; author and Educational Explorers Ltd for an extract from *One off* by Tom Johnson, from the 'My Life and My Work' Series; the Executors of the James Joyce Estate and Jonathan Cape Ltd for an extract from *Portrait of the Artist as a Young Man* by James Joyce; Longman Group Ltd for an extract from *Eastern Windows* by F.D. Ommanney; the Editor of New Society for an extract from 'Social Survey— Religion' from *New Society* 27th May 1965; Thomas Nelson & Sons Ltd for an adapted extract from *Newspapers*: Mass Media Series by R.B. Heath. Nelson, London 1968; Penguin Books Ltd. for an extract from *Alcoholism* by N. Kessel and H. Walton, an extract from *British Herbs* by F. Ransom and an extract from *War and Peace* by L.N. Tolstoy, translated by Rosemary Edmonds; A.D. Peters and Co. for an extract from *Scoop* by Evelyn Waugh; author's agents for an extract from *Ross* by Terence Rattigan; author for an extract from *Venereal Disease—A Simple Explanation* by Philip S. Silver, MRCS, LRCP; The Sunday Times for statistics of 'Britain's Labour Force' from the Business News section of *The Sunday Times* 5th September, 1965 and statistics from 'The World of Crisis Points' from *The Sunday Times Magazine* 31st March, 1974; Thomas Tait & Sons Ltd for their leaflet entitled *A Very Brief Description of Paper-making*; The Press Office and Information Centre (USIS) for extracts from 'College Students of the 1960s' quoted by Dr. R.S. Pitkin in *Young America*; author's agents and Martin Secker and Warburg Ltd for an extract from Act III of *The Night of the Iguana* by Tennessee Williams; Harvey Unna Ltd for an extract from Jack Pulman's television adaptation of *War and Peace*; author's agents for 'Pot' by Wayland Young from The Guardian 23rd October 1963. © Wayland Young, 1963 and Yugotours Ltd for extracts adapted from *Yugotours Holiday* ABC and *Yugotours Holiday Brochure*.

Photographs and illustration material are reproduced by permission of the following: Aerofilms, page 82; Automobile Association, page 66; B.B.C., pages 208 and 209; British Tourist Authority, page 70; British Travel Association, page 126; J. Allan Cash, pages 158, 193 and 196; Chichester Festival Theatre, pages 114 and 116; Cogent Elliot Ltd., page 76; G. Cuallado, page 118; John Gay, pages 32 and 166; John Goldblatt, pages 31 and 52; Heron Books Ltd., page 176; Michael Hollist, pages 6 and 7; Interlink Public Relations Ltd., pages 94 and 95; I.P.C. Magazines, page 178; Keystone Press, page 102; Percy Lund, Humphries and Co. Ltd., pages 27 and 28; Mercedes-Benz, page 128; Ministry of Public Building and Works, page 104; Janine Niepce, pages 30, 194, 195, 197 and 198; Syndication International, pages 4, 33, 58, 64, 92, 120, 135, 136, 141, 142, 159, 168, 180 and 201; United States Information Service, 56, 72, 124, 152 and 202; Valentine and Sons Ltd., page 115; Rein Valme, page 42; Ward Lock and Co. Ltd., page 48; Janine Wiedel, pages 21, 22, 40, 80 and 83.

It is to be noted that the Army Apprentices School charts reproduced on page 38 are not in current use.

Foreword

The aim of this book is to present a series of assignments, based on and related to selected photographs, diagrams and extracts, which will enable students in the upper forms of secondary schools and colleges of further education to practise their powers of understanding and expression.

Much of the work is based upon the belief that the power of expression springs from the art of observation, and that the visual image can be used to encourage such observation and so lead to effective writing.

The arrangement of the assignments offers maximum variety and interest, and some progression according to difficulty. As the book does not take the form of a conventional course a Reference Section is provided to enable the student to check on those skills which may have been taught but are not yet fully mastered.

There is sufficient practice material for a two-year course and ample scope for exposition, discussion and further reading at the discretion of the tutor.

Contents *(Figures refer to page numbers)*

I

Read the following poem carefully, and then:

(*a*) tell the story in your own words, and

(*b*) write a brief criticism of it, saying whether you think it is a good poem or a bad one and giving reasons for your view.

Out, Out . . .

The buzz saw snarled and rattled in the yard
And made dust and dropped stove-length sticks of wood,
Sweet-scented stuff when the breeze drew across it.
And from there those that lifted eyes could count
Five mountain ranges one behind the other
Under the sunset far into Vermont.
And the saw snarled and rattled, snarled and rattled,
As it ran light, or had to bear a load.
And nothing happened: day was all but done.
Call it a day, I wish they might have said
To please the boy by giving him the half hour
That a boy counts so much when saved from work.
His sister stood beside them in her apron
To tell them 'Supper'. At the word, the saw,
As if to prove saws knew what supper meant,
Leaped out of the boy's hand, or seemed to leap—
He must have given the hand. However it was,
Neither refused the meeting. But the hand!
The boy's first outcry was a rueful laugh,
As he swung toward them holding up the hand
Half in appeal, but half as if to keep
The life from spilling. Then the boy saw all—
Since he was old enough to know, big boy
Doing a man's work, though a child at heart—
He saw all spoiled. 'Don't let him cut my hand off—
The doctor, when he comes. Don't let him sister!'
So. But the hand was gone already.
The doctor put him in the dark of ether.

He lay and puffed his lips out with his breath.
And then—the watcher at his pulse took fright.
No one believed. They listened at his heart.
Little—less—nothing—and that ended it.
No more to build on there. And they, since they
Were not the one dead, turned to their affairs.

ROBERT FROST

2

Use the photograph and the following information to write a narrative account of the incident as told by the watchman who discovered the fire and stayed to help the firemen.

1 The fire began at 5.30 pm and was discovered by a watchman.
2 Flames 100 feet high shot above the building.
3 All Manchester fire brigades were mobilised and more than 100 jets were used.
4 Hundreds of firemen tried to save the store and the buildings near by.
5 Twelve firemen were treated for minor injuries.
6 Damage was estimated at hundreds of thousands of pounds.
7 The fire was still blazing over four hours later, but the danger of the fire spreading had been averted.

You are a newspaper reporter accompanying the press photographer who took these pictures in Israel. They show a young policewoman directing traffic and people at a multi-junction in the heart of Jerusalem.

Your Editor wants three paragraphs to go with the photographs for a half-page feature called Photonews. Supply a title, make up any names or information you need and write the paragraphs for him.

4

Read the following passage carefully and then make a summary of it in not more than 120 words. You are advised to read the information given on page 220 of the Reference Section before you begin.

No archaeological excavation has ever excited so general and so lasting an interest as that which brought to light the tomb of the Pharaoh Tutankhamun. The tomb's importance was due, first and foremost, to the amazing number of beautiful things which it contained—an unparalleled contribution to the world's treasury of art which the public was right to appreciate.

On the other hand it must be admitted that the discovery added nothing to what was known about the history of Egypt. The tomb yielded no written documents other than the stereotyped funerary inscriptions. The brief reign of this insignificant boy Pharaoh (he was only eighteen years old when he died) was not marked by any event of note; that he renounced the Aten worship proclaimed by his father-in-law Akhenaton and that under his rule the priests of Amun at Thebes regained their old power was a fact already familiar to historians. Of course the tomb, the only Egyptian royal tomb found virtually intact, did illustrate with unsurpassed splendour the ritual of a Pharaoh's burial, but ritual too was already known, from written documents, from wall-paintings and reliefs, and from objects surviving in plundered graves; it was indeed satisfactory to have the actual furniture instead of pictures of it, but it taught us nothing new.

What struck the imagination of the world was, in the first place, the dramatic character of the discovery—the long and patient search, a real act of faith, culminating in the discovery of something the like of which had never been found before—the undisturbed body of one of the ancient Egyptian kings. Egypt had always figured as the land of mystery and romance, and here was romance brought to life. In the second place there was the sensational prodigality of the treasures which today fill room after room of the Cairo Museum. It was a curiously mixed collection. Side by side with objects of breath-taking beauty there were others exhibiting a quite lamentable taste; on the one hand there was superfine technique, on the other, careless and shoddy workmanship. But in the excitement of the moment the public could not stop to discriminate but accepted everything alike as marvellous; the name of Tutankhamun, which had hitherto meant little even to the professional Egyptologist, became 'familiar as a household word' throughout

Europe and America. It can be fairly said that this popular reaction was the main contribution to archaeology made by the famous tomb.

SIR LEONARD WOOLLEY *History Unearthed*

5

A magazine carried out a nationwide survey to discover whether or not people wanted their children taught about God in school. Imagine that one of the interviewers has called at your house and requires an answer to each of the following five questions. Write down the answer you would give and in each case supply a good reason for the answer.

The Questions

1 By and large, do you think of Britain as a Christian country or not?
2 All schoolchildren have to take part in religious instruction and daily worship unless their parents ask for them to be excused. Do you think this arrangement should continue or not?
3 Would you prefer religious instruction to compare different religions, or to concentrate on Christianity?
4 Would you prefer there to be no religious instruction in state primary schools?
5 Would you prefer there to be no religious instruction in state secondary schools?

6

Study the specimen letter given on page 219 of the Reference Section and then write a suitable letter of application in reply to the advertisement below.

THE ROTEM CORPORATION LIMITED
MANUFACTURERS OF HIGH-PRESSURE COUPLINGS

Careers in Commerce

Applications are invited from young men and young women due to leave school at the end of the summer term who are interested in making a career in the light engineering industry. The candidates must be 16/17 years of age and be educated to GCE O Level or CSE Grade I. Training will be carried out in all departments of the Company and will include day release for further study. The training period is for two years.

Written applications in the first instance to:

The Personnel Manager
The Rotem Corporation Ltd
Star Works, Hargreaves Road
Portsmouth

7

Turn to the Reference Section and revise the process of note-making. Now make notes on the following passage using the specimen notes on page 224 as a guide.

Originally the Opium Poppy came from the East—Persia, India and China—but it has been cultivated for centuries in Europe, and spread to Britain many years ago.

This lovely plant has greyish-green leaves, and tall, stout stalks from which swing the green buds, later to be succeeded by a quickly passing flower. The plump heads are greenish-white, soon ripening to light brown. Poppies prefer a rich, moist, well-cultivated soil, which is one reason why they thrive so well in our herbaceous borders. A clump or row of them in the herb-garden will provide a pleasant patch of colour during the summer, but ruthless measures must be taken in cutting the seed-heads.

Opium is extracted from the unripe heads, cuts being made in the outer skin, and the white, milky juice scraped out. This is formed into cakes and dried in the sun, when it becomes deep brown. Though the poppy has been cultivated in Britain since 1798, it has never been grown for the extraction of opium, as only plants grown in hot, sunny climates produce this drug.

Morphine, one of the world's most valuable medicines, is a product of opium, getting this name from Morpheus, the God of Sleep. But the poppy is also grown very largely for its heads, as they are employed in the making of sedative drugs for external inflammation and included in cough medicines. As the seeds do not contain morphine, they are used in European countries in confectionery, being sprinkled on cakes, rolls and bread, giving a faint spicy flavour.

Poppy-heads have long been a rural remedy for toothache, neuralgia and other nervous pains, and once it was common to see bunches of the dried heads hanging in chemists' shops. The poppy, as the source of many valuable alkaloids, is official in the *British Pharmacopoeia*.

FLORENCE RANSON *British Herbs*

8

Read the information and the extract, then answer the questions.

Friendship and Duty

Thomas Becket and King Henry II of England were very close friends. Becket became Archbishop of Canterbury at the King's command because Henry believed that through Becket he would be able to control the Church of England.

As Archbishop, Becket took his allegiance to God and the Church as a serious duty and found that he could not serve both God and the King. Henry felt betrayed and after a bitter quarrel Becket escaped to France in order to save his life and make an appeal to the Pope.

Eventually the King of France was able to persuade the two men to make their peace with each other. This scene, taken from *Becket* by Jean Anouilh, records their first meeting after the quarrel and separation.

When the lights come up, Becket and the King, on horseback, are alone in the middle of a vast, arid plain, facing each other. Becket is right of the King. Throughout the episode the winter blizzard wails like a shrill dirge beneath their words. And during their silences only the wind is heard.

KING: You look older, Thomas.

BECKET: You, too, Highness. Are you sure you aren't too cold?

KING: I'm frozen stiff. You love it, of course. You're in your element, aren't you? And you're barefooted, as well.

BECKET (*smiling*): That's my latest affectation.

KING: Even with these fur boots on, my chilblains are killing me. Aren't yours, or don't you have any?

BECKET (*gently*): Of course.

KING (*crackling*): You're offering them up to God, I hope, holy monk?

BECKET (*gravely*): I have better things to offer Him.

KING (*with a sudden cry*): If we start straight away, we're sure to quarrel. Let's talk about trivial things. You know my son is fourteen? He's come of age.

BECKET: Has he improved at all?

KING: He's a little idiot and sly like his mother. Becket, don't ever marry.

BECKET (*smiling*): The matter has been taken out of my hands. By your Highness. It was you who had me ordained.

KING (*with a cry*): Let's not start yet, I tell you. Talk about something else.

BECKET (*lightly*): Has your Highness done much hunting lately?

KING (*snarling*): Yes, every day. And it doesn't amuse me any more.

BECKET: Have you any new hawks?

KING (*furiously*): The most expensive on the market. But they don't fly straight.

BECKET: And your horses?

KING: The Sultan sent me four superb stallions for the tenth anniversary of my reign. But they throw everyone. Nobody has managed to mount one of them, yet.

BECKET (*smiling*): I must see what I can do about that some day.

KING: They'll throw you too. And we'll see your buttocks under your robe. At least I hope so, or everything would be too dismal.

BECKET (*after a pause*): Do you know what I miss most, Sire? The horses.

KING: And the women?

BECKET (*simply*): I've forgotten.

KING: You hypocrite! You turned into a hypocrite when you became a priest. (*Abruptly*) Did you love Gwendolen?

BECKET: I've forgotten her, too.

KING: You did love her. That's the only way I can account for it.

BECKET (*gravely*): No, my prince, in my soul and conscience, I did not love her.

KING: Then you never loved anything—that's worse. (*Churlishly*) Why are you calling me your prince, like in the old days?

BECKET (*gently*): Because you have remained my prince.

KING (*crying out*): Then why are you doing me harm?

BECKET (*gently*): Let's talk about something else.

KING: Well, what? I'm cold.

BECKET: I always told you, my prince, that one must fight the cold with the cold's own weapons. Strip naked and splash yourself with cold water every morning.

KING: I used to, when you were there to force me into it. I never wash now. I stink. I grew a beard at one time. Did you know?

BECKET (*smiling*): Yes. I had a good laugh over it.

KING: I cut it off, because it itched. (*He cries out suddenly, like a lost child*) Becket, I'm bored.

BECKET (*gravely*): My prince. I do so wish I could help you.

KING: Then what are you waiting for? You can see I'm dying for it.

BECKET (*quietly*): I'm waiting for the honour of God and the honour of the King to become one.

KING: You'll wait a long time, then.

BECKET: Yes. I'm afraid I will.

(*There is a pause. Only the wind is heard*)

KING (*suddenly*): If we've nothing more to say to each other, we might as well go and get warm.

BECKET: We have everything to say to each other, my prince. The opportunity may not occur again.

KING: Make haste, then. Or there'll be two frozen statues making their peace in a frozen eternity. I am your King, Becket. And so long as we are on this earth, you owe me the first move. I'm prepared to forget a lot of things, but not the fact that I am King. You yourself taught me that.

BECKET (*gravely*): Never forget it, my prince. Even against God. You have a different task to do. You have to steer the ship.

KING: And you—what do you have to do?

BECKET: Resist you with all my might, when you steer against the wind.

KING: Do you expect the wind to be behind me, Becket? No such luck! That's fairy-tale navigation. God on the King's side? That's never happened yet. It's a head-on wind. And there must be somebody to keep the watch.

BECKET: And somebody else to direct the wind for God. The tasks have been shared out, once and for all. The pity of it is that it should have been between us two, my prince—who were friends.

Comprehension, Interpretation and Comment

1 Why has Anouilh set this scene in the middle of a plain with Becket and the King as two isolated figures?

2 What impression is conveyed by the sounds of the winter blizzard and the wind? Is there anything in the text to support this impression?

3 Why does the King wish to talk about trivial things? Name four of the trivial things covered in the conversation.

4 The King gives several reasons why he is no longer amused by hunting. Name a reason he did not give.

5 Note the acting directions for the King—*crackling, with a sudden cry, snarling, furiously, abruptly, churlishly, cries out suddenly, like a lost child.* Why does the King behave in this manner?

15

6 Write three or four sentences explaining Becket's attitude towards the King.

7 BECKET: Yes. I'm afraid I will.

(*There is a pause. Only the wind is heard.*)

Why is the pause and the sound effect introduced at this point?

8 'The tasks have been shared out, once and for all.' Explain in your own words the tasks which were bigger than the friendship of the two men.

9 Read the scene again and make notes on the characters of the two men. Write two short passages which give the characters of both Henry and Becket as they are revealed in this scene.

9

The following tables represent the replies to a group of questions about the leisure habits of children in three age groups. Study the figures carefully and then write a report for each age group on the habits revealed. It would be wise to read 'The Interpretation of Statistics' on page 227 before you begin.

1 What time did your child go to bed last night?

Age	5–7	8–10	11–13
	%	%	%
7 pm or earlier	16	—	1
Between 7 and 8 pm	48	29	9
Between 8 and 9 pm	25	49	47
After 9 pm	8	20	40
Don't know	3	2	3
	100	100	100

2 How much time did he spend yesterday playing out of doors?

Age	5–7	8–10	11–13
	%	%	%
No time at all	6	8	14
One hour or less	4	8	7
Over 1 hour–3 hours	30	27	17
Over 3 hours–5 hours	23	21	26
Over 5 hours–7 hours	20	18	21
Over 7 hours	10	13	10
Don't know	7	5	5
	100	100	100

3 How much time did he spend yesterday doing homework?

Age	5-7	8-10	11-13
	%	%	%
No time at all	74	67	53
Half hour or less	18	21	13
Over ½ hour–2 hours	4	8	22
Over 2 hours	—	—	4
Don't know	4	4	8
	100	100	100

4 How much time did your child spend watching television yesterday?

Age	5-7	8-10	11-13
	%	%	%
No time at all	20	12	10
One hour or less	39	34	27
Over 1 hour up to 2	26	28	28
Over 2 hours up to 3	6	12	11
Over 3 hours	6	10	19
Don't know	3	4	5
	100	100	100

5 How often does he go to the cinema?

	%
Once a week or more often	22
Once a fortnight	4
Once a month	9
Less often than once a month	37
Never	28
	100

6 During the past week has your child stayed up beyond his usual bedtime to see a particular television programme?

	DURING TERM TIME	DURING HOLIDAYS
	%	%
Yes	42	50
No	58	50
	100	100

from *Parents, Children and Television.* HMSO

IO

Study the following graph and then write a short article telling how electricity requirements fluctuate throughout a winter and a summer day.

Source: *Power Progress* Central Electricity Generating Board

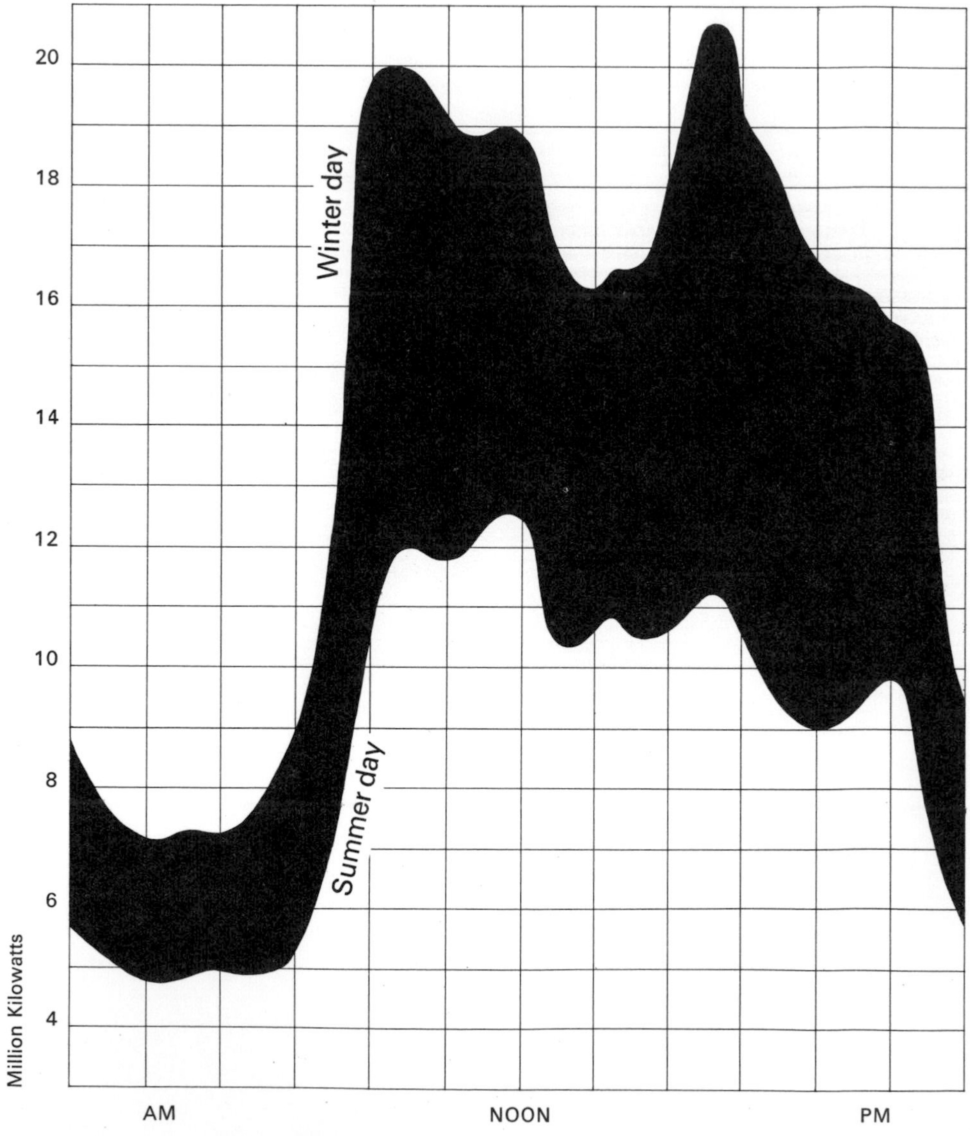

Study this picture of American graffiti artists at work and then answer the questions which follow.

1 Describe in not more than 100 words the section of the wall shown in the photograph.
2 How can you tell that the painting of the wall was planned and not carried out on the spur of the moment?
3 Write a general description of the artists as a group. Work directly from the photograph and search for the exact words that seem to fit.
4 Imagine that you are one of the artists. Write a paragraph in which you explain why you are painting the wall.
5 This picture is to appear in an underground newspaper feature called Topix. Make up any further information you need to write a short factual account to accompany it.
6 The story of the incident is to be printed in a college newspaper under the title 'The Day We Painted The Wall'. Write the full story as if you were the organiser.

12

1 Extract further information from this photograph to complete the following set of notes.

Shopping in Greenland

I STORE
    a Owner
    b Construction

II PEOPLE
    a Type
    b Age
    c Sex
    d Dress

III PURCHASES
    a Food
    b Other goods

2 Write a factual description of this picture using the notes you have made as a basis for your work.

13

Turn to page 227 and read 'The Interpretation of Statistics'. Use this method to state in the form of a short article the facts conveyed by the following figures and the inferences you would draw from them.

Children of all ages in special schools in England and Wales

	BOYS	GIRLS	TOTAL
blind	566	465	1,031
partially sighted	1,319	747	2,066
deaf	1,893	1,539	3,452
partially hearing	1,178	919	2,097
physically handicapped	5,716	4,115	9,831
delicate	3,403	2,151	5,554
maladjusted	6,966	1,986	8,952
educationally subnormal	45,894	31,707	77,601
epileptic	744	515	1,259
speech defect	1,215	599	1,814
in-hospital schools	5,106	3,520	8,626
totals	74,000	48,283	122,283

14

1 Write a suitable letter of application in reply to one of the advertisements below. Use the address of your local paper.
2 Write a letter to some person of influence who knows you, asking him for a testimonial to enclose with your application.

The Windsor Echo

SITUATIONS VACANT

YOUNG MAN wanted for statistical work by large manufacturer. Good education, quick at figures, and capable of working on his own initiative. Apply the Manager, Box C. 187.

GIRL required, school leaver considered, good at figures, for wages department of small firm. State age, previous experience (if any) and when free to start to Box G. 58.

APPRENTICE required for lithographic printer. Three months probation period, five years apprenticeship. Day release to School of Printing and Graphic Art. Apply to Box FR. 91.

TRAINEE TRACER wanted by electronics firm. Girl or boy. Write about yourself to Box P. 69.

GIRL FRIDAY wanted for office department of local estate agent. Super job for young girl aged 16+, to do some typing, lots of telephone work and general office responsibilities. Good salary plus LVs. Apply Box T. 34.

15

Nature News is a new magazine for children which seeks to interest the average boy or girl in this subject. The Editor requires a 400-word article on the Douglas fir for his first issue and has asked you to write it.

Study the basic information, drawings and photograph on the following two pages and supplement this with information from the school or local library. Make suitable notes and work out the best order for the presentation of the facts.

In this type of article, your English should be plain and straightforward. Use simple sentences rather than long and involved ones. It may help if you think of a particular reader for whom you are writing; one who knows less about the subject than you do but who is not completely ignorant.

Douglas Fir *Pseudotsuga Douglasii* Introduced into Britain in 1872

Douglas fir is very variable in type, but it makes a fine specimen when grown in suitable positions. The timber is valuable and it has been used chiefly as a forest tree in this country, but it is beautiful when grown in the open and might be used more often in that way for its ornamental value and on account of its quick growth. Under forest conditions its outstanding feature is the great height of straight bole, free of branches and tapering very gradually.

Planting Small plants under 1 metre high transplant best. Early autumn or late spring.

Growth Fast growing, often exceeding 60 cm a year for the first twenty or thirty years. Very tall and graceful, Douglas fir is a long-lived tree and may reach a height of over 100 metres and a diameter of 5.5 metres when many hundreds of years old. The main stem persists to the tip of the tree and the lateral branches are comparativel slender and slightly drooping.

Soil Moist soils of many types. Only in very mois atmospheric conditions can Douglas fir endure dr sandy soils. It will grow on moist acid soils and ever on the edge of brackish water.

Climate In Britain, Douglas fir is extremely hardy against frost, but dislikes very windy positions. I enjoys the moist atmosphere of our western and northern zones.

Habitat This tree is found on the Pacific coast from British Columbia to Mexico and inland as far as the east side of the Rockies, in some parts up to an altitude of 6,000 feet. Forests of pure Douglas fir are found and it also occurs in mixed woods.

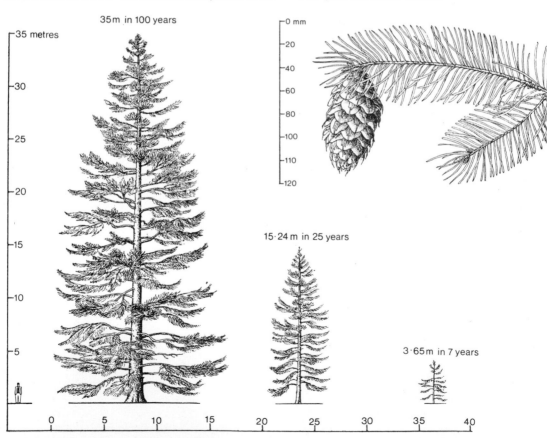

35m in 100 years

15·24 m in 25 years

3·65m in 7 years

16

The pictures in this section have been selected to provide you with written work on the description of faces.

Study the pictures one at a time and make notes on the shape of the face, hair style, size of features, texture of skin, profile and expression. Note the lines on a face, the curve of a mouth and the glint of an eye. Follow a definite order and finish with one feature before you pass to the next.

Decide what is the main impression—confident, gloomy, carefree, sly, resigned —and draw attention to the features that convey this impression. Search for words that best capture the meaning of an expression or best describe a feature with precision. Avoid sentences that do no more than name the feature, eg: 'The young girl's eyes are bright . . .' Point out, if possible, how the feature reveals the person's character, and describe what it reminds you of, eg: 'Her eyes are bright with a dancing gaiety; like the sparkle of sun on water.'

1 Write a description of each of the faces in this section.
2 Write a short character sketch of the young man on page 31.
3 Write a short story or a scene from a play and introduce as characters two or more of the people in this section.

17

Read the following passage carefully, then answer the questions.

The Clark's Fork Valley, Wyoming

At the end of summer, the big trout would be out in the centre of the stream; they were leaving the pools along the upper part of the river and dropping down to spend the winter in the deep water of the canyon. It was wonderful fly-fishing then in the first weeks of September. The native trout were sleek, shining, and heavy, and nearly all of them leaped when they took the fly. If you fished two flies, you would often have two big trout on and the need to handle them very delicately in that heavy current.

The nights were cold, and, if you woke in the night, you would hear the coyotes. But you did not want to get out on the stream too early in the day because the nights were so cold they chilled the water, and the sun had to be on the river until almost noon before the trout would start to feed.

You could ride in the morning, or sit in front of the cabin, lazy in the sun, and look across the valley where the hay was cut so the meadows were cropped brown and smooth to the line of quaking aspens along the river, now turning yellow in the fall. And on the hills rising beyond, the sage was silvery grey.

Up the river were the two peaks of Pilot and Index, where we would hunt mountain-sheep later in the month, and you sat in the sun and marvelled at the formal, clean-lined shape mountains can have at a distance, so that you remember them in the shapes they show from far away, and not as the broken rock-slides you crossed, the jagged edges you pulled up by, and the narrow shelves you sweated along, afraid to look down, to round that peak that looked so smooth and geometrical. You climbed around it to come out on a clear space to look down to where an old ram and three young rams were feeding in the juniper bushes in a high, grassy pocket cupped against the broken rock of the peak.

The old ram was purple-grey, his rump was white, and when he raised his head you saw the great heavy curl of his horns. It was the white of his rump that had betrayed him to you in the green junipers when you had lain in the lee of a rock, out of the wind, three miles away, looking carefully at every yard of the high country through a pair of good Zeiss glasses.

Now as you sat in front of the cabin, you remembered that down-hill shot and the young rams standing, their heads turned, staring at him, waiting for him to get up. They could not see you on that high ledge, nor wind you, and the shot made no more impression on them than a boulder falling.

You remembered the year we had built a cabin at the head of Timber Creek, and the big grizzly that tore it open every time we were away. The snow came later that year, and this bear would not hibernate, but spent his autumn tearing open cabins and ruining a trap-line. But he was so smart you never saw him in the day. Then you remembered coming on the three grizzlies in the high country at the head of Crandall Creek. You heard a crash of timber and thought it was a cow elk bolting, and then there they were, in the broken shadow, running with an easy, lurching smoothness, the afternoon sun making their coats a soft, bristling silver.

You remembered elk bugling in the fall, the bull so close you could see his chest muscles swell as he lifted his head, and still not see his head in the thick timber; but hear that deep, high mounting whistle and the answer from across another valley. You thought of all the heads you had turned down and refused to shoot, and you were pleased.

You remembered how this country had looked when you first came into it. You could remember all the hunting and all the fishing and the riding in the summer sun and the dust of the pack-train, the silent riding in the hills in the sharp cold of fall going up after the cattle on the high range, finding them wild as deer and as quiet, only bawling noisily when they were all herded together being forced along down into the lower country.

Then there was the winter; the trees bare now, the snow blowing so you could not see, the saddle wet, then frozen as you came downhill, breaking a trail through the snow, trying to keep your legs moving, and the sharp, warming taste of whiskey when you hit the ranch and changed your clothes in front of the big open fireplace. It's a good country.

ERNEST HEMINGWAY *The Clark's Fork Valley, Wyoming*

Comprehension, Interpretation and Comment

1 Why were there so many trout in the centre of the stream during the first weeks of September?
2 Describe the sequence of events which led to the shooting of the old ram without the young rams realising it.

3 Give the names of two animals which are mentioned in paragraphs preceding the ones in which they are described.
4 During which season of the year were the cattle on the high range brought down into the valley?
5 Hemingway feels that this is a good country. Would it be a good country for you? Give your reasons.
6 Write a brief description of the author as he reveals himself in this passage.
7 Clark's Fork Valley is described here from a particular point of view. Other people describing the valley might choose to emphasise a different aspect. Use the information given in the passage to describe the valley as an artist might see it. Make the description as full, as accurate, and as vivid as you can.

18

Read the following passage carefully, give it a title, decide what are its main points, add subheadings and collect information under those headings.

The Giant's Causeway is one of the natural wonders of the world, and lies on the northern coast of Ireland, near Portrush in the county of Antrim. It consists of thousands of columns of reddish basalt rock, generally six-sided, set closely together in a honeycomb formation. The columns differ in height, and form in the Grand Causeway a sort of giant staircase leading down to the sea. There are picturesque and grotesque formations, such as the Giant's Organ, where the columns rise high into the air, reminding the onlooker of the pipes of a great church organ. The Wishing Chair is built of a single pillar surrounded by higher pillars, giving it the shape of an arm-chair.

There are many legends which attempt to explain the origin of the Giant's Causeway, the most popular being that Finn MacCool, a legendary Irish giant, built it in order to cross to the Scottish Coast.

Geologists say that it was caused by the rapid cooling and cracking of a sheet of basalt, which poured over the land from a fissure eruption in the Tertiary Geological Period several million years ago. Most of the basalt columns are six-sided, but there is one—the keystone—with three sides, and a few others with seven, eight, and nine sides.

Oxford Junior Encyclopaedia, Vol. III, p. 189

Army Apprentices College/Arborfield
ONC Student Technicians

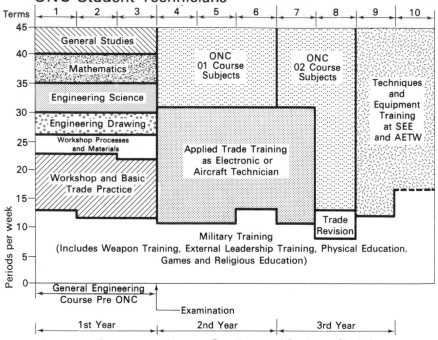

Terms: 1 | 2 | 3 | 4 | 5 | 6 | 7 | 8 | 9 | 10

Periods per week (0–45)

- General Studies
- Mathematics
- Engineering Science
- Engineering Drawing
- Workshop Processes and Materials
- Workshop and Basic Trade Practice
- ONC 01 Course Subjects
- ONC 02 Course Subjects
- Techniques and Equipment Training at SEE and AETW
- Applied Trade Training as Electronic or Aircraft Technician
- Trade Revision
- Military Training (Includes Weapon Training, External Leadership Training, Physical Education, Games and Religious Education)

General Engineering Course Pre ONC
← Examination

1st Year | 2nd Year | 3rd Year

Army Apprentices College/Arborfield
City and Guilds Artisan Students

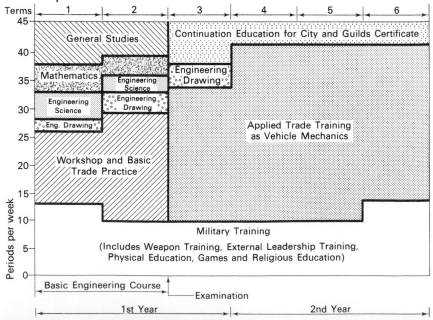

Terms: 1 | 2 | 3 | 4 | 5 | 6

Periods per week (0–45)

- General Studies
- Continuation Education for City and Guilds Certificate
- Mathematics
- Engineering Science
- Engineering Drawing
- Eng. Drawing
- Workshop and Basic Trade Practice
- Applied Trade Training as Vehicle Mechanics
- Military Training (Includes Weapon Training, External Leadership Training, Physical Education, Games and Religious Education)

Basic Engineering Course
← Examination

1st Year | 2nd Year

19

The diagrams on the opposite page show the time given to various activities on two courses at an Army Apprentices College. Study them carefully and then answer the questions below.

1 Give the length of the courses in years, the number of terms per course and the number of periods worked each week.
2 How many hours per week do students spend in training? (Each period is forty minutes long.)
3 Which is the longer of the two courses? Why do you think this is so?
4 Name three activities that are common to the first two terms of both courses.
5 Which activity continues throughout both courses?
6 State, for each course, the year and term in which most periods are devoted to Workshop and Basic Trade Practice.
7 On which course is more time given to Applied Trade Training?
8 Estimate the number of periods per week devoted to (a) General Studies, and (b) Mathematics, in the first year of each course.
9 Which course would you be taking if you were studying Aeronautics in terms seven and eight of the third year?
10 When do the City and Guilds Artisan Students have their Military Training increased at the expense of other activities?
11 When do ONC Student Technicians take their examination?
12 Compare the two courses and then write down any significant differences you are able to find.

20

A good title is short and effective. It summarises, either directly or by suggestion, the most important idea, action or emotion in a picture or a piece of writing.

Study the photograph and write down several single words which could be used as a title. Then try with a list of phrases of four or five words each. Study your efforts and select the word or phrase which you consider to be the most accurate as a title for the photograph.

Write a description of the scene using your title. It is wise to work to a plan in order to avoid jumping from one person to another. Start with a paragraph about the teacher and make him your central point. When you write paragraphs for each of the pupils, explain their position in the group as being beside or behind him. Complete your description of each person in a single paragraph.

21

This photograph was taken in Stockholm where the camera caught the reactions of two women who were watching a young couple kiss in public.

1 Supply a title for the photograph.
2 Write as much as you can about the woman on the right. Clues to her character can be obtained from the eyes, the spectacles, the lips, the dress, the jewellery, and the position of the handbag.
3 Think of a reason for their attitudes.
4 What might the woman on the left be saying? Give her companion's answer.
5 Supply appropriate names for the women and develop the last question into a conversation between them on the manners of young people in public. Before you write, imagine who these two women are, what they are thinking, what they are feeling, and what their voices would sound like. Treat the conversation as a scene from a play using the extract from *Becket* (page 13) as an example. If it is necessary, place in brackets after each speech an indication of how the words should be spoken.
6 Imagine that you were the boy or the girl who was doing the kissing in public. Write a short defence of your action.

22

Much of the advertising in modern society is concerned with giving information about goods and services for sale, and this type of advertising might be called 'informational'. There is a great deal of informational advertising in our streets, in local daily and weekly newspapers, in trade and technical magazines, and in the classified advertisements of the national daily newspapers.

Advertisements which appear on television, or the display advertisements of the mass circulation magazines and the daily and Sunday newspapers, may be of a different nature. This type of advertisement offers very little information and sets out quite deliberately to work upon the emotions, the mental attitudes and the subconscious mind of the viewer or reader. Some of this persuasive advertising is very sophisticated and complex, but clear examples at a simple level can be seen in the names given by manufacturers to their products.

1 Study the following names of paint shades and then answer the questions below.

Manor Grey	Cocoon	Rainbow Green
Zephyr	Dawn Pink	Windsor Grey
Balmoral Blue	Limelight	Medium Chartreuse
Medici Green	Cheer	Icefall
Buttermilk	Cream	Post Office Red
Soft Mystic Blue	Pink Haze	Blue Delight
Antique Cream	Mayflower	Buckingham Green
Pale Art Grey	Veronica	Louis XIV Green
Opera Pink	Pink Show	Lavender
Bitter Lime	Carnival	Mauve Sheen
Parchment	Foxglove	Sandalwood
Buena Vista	White Beach	Tea Rose
Wild Gorse	Diane Pink	Candy Shimmer

(a) Write down the names from the list that give no indication of the colour.

(b) Select and write down the names which place the colour in a flattering relationship to:

I art;
II natural beauty;
III culture;
IV royalty.

(c) Write down the names of the colours (usually pinks and blues) that might appeal to the dreams and fantasies of the subconscious mind.

(d) The British Standards Institution has an official number for each paint colour (eg Mimosa—B.S. 4.055) and manufacturers could use these numbers in order to identify their colours. Why do they prefer names and what are the names trying to do in addition to identifying the colour?

2 All of us link words together in our minds and a particular word may set off a train of other words, or start an emotional reaction, or link up with one of our mental attitudes. Many product names are chosen because of their image and the association which the name conjures up. Look at the following brand names for cigarettes and for each one write down the first four words that come into your mind.

Everest	Guards	St. Moritz
Perfectos	Rembrandt	Buckingham
Silk Cut	Nelson	Sotheby's

Study your responses and then write down, for each group of four words, the idea or image that has been built into the brand name.

3 Repeat this exercise using the following model names of cars.

Victor	Phantom	Avenger
Interceptor	Scimitar	Consul
Marathon	Hunter	Allegro

4 Study the following groups of names given to lipstick shades and then write a sentence or two about the overall impression conveyed by each group.

Group One	Group Two	Group Three
Pretty Pink	Entice	Melting Point
Tender Pink	Double O Seven	Hot Red
Natural Pink	Pink Witch	Swamp Fire
Dew Pink	Wild Cat	Flashpoint
Dawn Pink	Fatal Pink	Fire Dance

23

Summarise the following passage, using your own words and reducing it to about one-third of its present length.

The first colour magazine as a supplement to a British newspaper was launched by the *Sunday Times* in 1962. It was not a new idea, for the distribution of a magazine with the Sunday newspaper was already established in the United States and Canada. The British version proved to be a better publication because it was superior in its use of paper and colour, and also in its content.

The magazine had a slow first year and then became such a success that the *Observer* was forced to follow suit with its own version. The third colour magazine to be launched was the *Weekend Telegraph* (now *The Daily Telegraph Magazine*). This magazine was tied to the *Sunday Telegraph* but was distributed with the Friday issue of the *Daily Telegraph* because its sales were larger.

The combined circulation of these three magazines has now reached over 30 million copies. Surveys show that more people read them than actually buy the parent newspaper. This arises because buyers of the newspaper pass the magazine on to friends or to such places as waiting rooms and hotel lounges.

How is it possible for a magazine to be given away as part of a newspaper? Who pays for the high cost of paper, colour-printing and staff? Quite simply, the money is obtained from advertising. A magazine can be given away if it attracts enough advertising to cover the cost of its production.

As costs are high it is necessary to charge much higher advertising rates than those for ordinary newspaper advertisements. But these premium rates can only apply if the magazine reaches people in an upper income group who have money to spend. It follows that colour magazines are distributed by quality newspapers whose readership is in this group and only then if the circulation is high enough. For example, the *Daily Telegraph* is able to distribute a magazine but the *Guardian* cannot because its circulation figure is too low. It is therefore unlikely that the popular daily and Sunday newspapers will be going into the colour magazine field. The *Daily Mirror* did make an attempt some years ago but it was shortlived and ended in disaster.

The primary function of a colour magazine is that of a carrier of advertising. It carries advertising just as the Post Office carries mail or trains carry passengers. Such cartage is profitable for it has been estimated that the advertising content of the three magazines is worth over £10 million per annum. The secondary function is to extend the feature pages of the newspaper and at the same time break new ground. A colour magazine offers an editor opportunities to experiment with colour and with pictorial journalism.

The content and nature of the three magazines are governed by the type of person who reads the parent newspapers, the content of other weekly magazines, and the fact that colour magazines go to press some three to six weeks before publication date.

The three newspapers concerned are read by the better educated and more sophisticated section of our population. This means that the content of the associated magazines is likely to consist of photographic reportage of cultural activities and of the contemporary scene.

The magazines tend also to avoid articles that infringe upon the ground covered by other weekly magazines bought by the public. For example, we do not get sequence pictures showing us how to achieve a particular hair style or how to modernise a bathroom. If colour magazines stray into this territory they do so with articles that are very general in their approach or which look at the subject from a very different angle.

Because of the time taken to produce colour magazines they rarely contain current news stories and topical background articles. Only when a future event is known can an article about it be included to appear when it takes place. In any case, current news stories and background articles should appear in the parent newspaper.

These three limiting factors ensure that the magazines fall between being news magazines and leisure magazines. They do not cover current news but concentrate on items of general interest to a particular group in our society. Their content is a hotch-potch of articles dealing with history, archaeology, science, cultural activities, fashion, travel, medicine, personalities, crime and cookery.

What of the future of colour magazines? Their great appeal to the advertiser has always been that he could use colour lavishly for his advertisements, and for this he was prepared to pay high rates. With the growth of TV colour advertising, however, he now has another choice. In addition, newspapers are now running full page colour advertisements. Colour magazines cannot exist without advertisements and if some of the advertising is switched to another medium they will have to turn to something new if they are to maintain their size or prevent themselves going out of circulation.

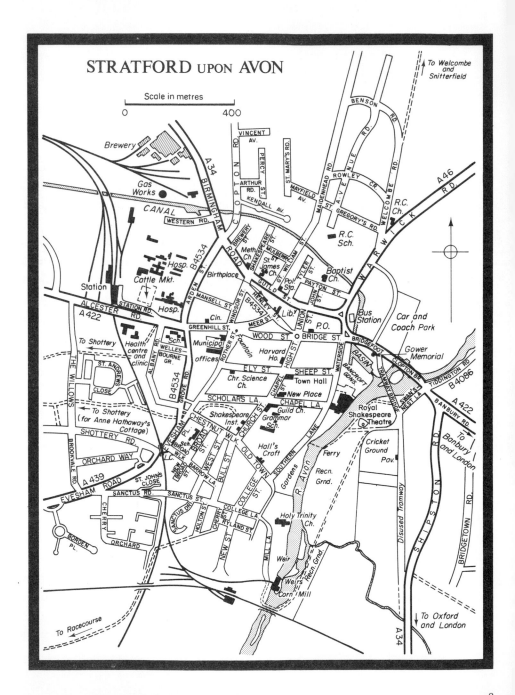

STRATFORD UPON AVON

24

Make a careful study of the plan of Stratford-upon-Avon and then answer the following questions.

1 List all 'A' class roads leaving the town and say where they lead.
2 A visitor to the town stopped you at the Holy Trinity Church and asked the way to Shakespeare's Birthplace. Give your reply.
3 Write a paragraph about the stretch of the river shown in the plan.
4 A friend is coming to Stratford-upon-Avon by train, but you are unable to meet him at the station. Write a letter apologising for this and explain how to get from the station to your house in Chapel Lane.
5 From your study of the plan write three paragraphs of general information about Stratford-upon-Avon.

25

Read the following passage and then answer the questions.

The Power of the Press

That afternoon Corker told William a great deal about the craft of journalism. The *Francmacon* weighed anchor, swung about and steamed into the ochre hills, through the straits and out into the open sea while Corker recounted the heroic legends of Fleet Street; he told of the classic scoops and hoaxes; of the confessions wrung from hysterical suspects; of the innuendo and intricate misrepresentations; the luscious, detailed inventions that composed contemporary history; of the positive, daring lies that got a chap a rise of screw, how Wenlock Jakes, highest paid journalist of the United States, scooped the world with an eye-witness story of the sinking of the *Lusitania* four hours before she was hit; how Hitchcock, the English Jakes, straddling over his desk in London, had chronicled day by day the horrors of the Messina earthquake; how Corker himself, not three months back, had had the rare good fortune to encounter a knight's widow trapped by the foot between lift and landing. 'It was through that story I got sent here,' said Corker. 'The boss promised me the first big chance that turned up. I little thought it would be this.'

Many of Corker's anecdotes dealt with the fabulous Wenlock Jakes. '. . . syndicated all over America. Gets a thousand dollars a week. When he turns up in a place you can bet your life that as long as he's there it'll be the news centre of the world.

'Why, once Jakes went out to cover a revolution in one of the Balkan capitals. He overslept in his carriage, woke up at the wrong station, didn't know any different, got out, went straight to a hotel, and cabled off a thousand word story about barricades in the streets, flaming churches, machine guns answering the rattle of his typewriter, a dead child, like a broken doll, spreadeagled in the deserted roadway below his window—*you* know.

'Well they were pretty surprised at his office, getting a story like that from the wrong country, but they trusted Jakes and splashed it in six national newspapers. That day every special in Europe got orders to rush to the new revolution. They arrived in shoals. Everything seemed quiet enough but it was as much as their jobs were worth to say so, with Jakes filing a thousand words of blood and thunder a day. So they chimed in too. Government stocks dropped, financial panic, state of emergency declared, army mobilized, famine, mutiny, and in less than a week there *was* an honest to God revolution under way, just as Jakes had said. There's the power of the press for you.'

EVELYN WAUGH *Scoop*

Comprehension and Interpretation

1 Suggest two interpretations of the word *craft* in the first sentence.
2 Explain clearly each of the following expressions as used in the first paragraph (use a dictionary if necessary):

classic scoops and hoaxes
confessions wrung from hysterical suspects
innuendo and intricate misrepresentations
the luscious, detailed inventions that composed contemporary history

3 What is the meaning of the word *screw* as it is used in the first paragraph? Write down two other slang expressions which mean the same thing.
4 What do we learn from the following about the methods of journalism practised by Wenlock Jakes?
'. . . how Wenlock Jakes, highest paid journalist of the United States, scooped the world with an eye-witness story of the sinking of the *Lusitania* four hours before she was hit; . . .'
5 Write a paragraph describing in your own words the impression you obtain of Fleet Street.
6 The story cabled by Wenlock Jakes contains several gaudy clichés of the type often found in newspaper reports of dramatic events. Write down what you consider to be the worst cliché in his story.
7 Write a brief character sketch of Wenlock Jakes.
8 Evelyn Waugh is a satirist who, in this passage, has caricatured and exaggerated the work of a journalist in order to drive home a particular point. What is the point he is making?
9 Thomas Jefferson believed in the power of the press. He once said: 'Were it left to me to decide whether we should have a government without newspapers, or newspapers without a government, I should not hesitate a moment to prefer the latter.' What are the dangers in having a government without newspapers?
10 Write the story of a journalist whose one thousand words a day caused a fifty-megaton bomb to explode over Paris. Use Wenlock Jakes and the last two paragraphs of the passage as models.

26

The woman in the photograph is a tour organiser and the man is a traveller who has put his wife on the wrong train.

1 Study the picture and try to imagine what these two people are like. What are they thinking? What are they feeling? What do their voices sound like? Whose fault is it that the wife is on the wrong train? Did the husband misunderstand or did the organiser give the wrong information? Write in play form the conversation which takes place between them. Choose language appropriate to each speaker and make the conversation lead up to a conclusion from what has been said. Your reader should finish with the feeling that, for the time being at least, the subject is over.

2 You are waiting for a train when this incident takes place. Describe the scene from the point of view of an onlooker. Pay particular attention to dress, faces, actions and tone of voice.

27

Read the following extract and then answer the questions that follow.

The Tender Trap

FRANCESCA (*rather huskily*): Alberto, why don't you get married? (*She pauses briefly*) After all, there comes a time when—naturally, one has to choose very carefully—among the people who are near to one. I know that there—*is* someone, certainly—who—in whom you could have complete confidence, and who has shown in the past how very reliable she can be—and how fond of you she really is.

ALBERTO (*laboriously hunting for a cigarette*): I—I'm not the boasting sort—but as a matter of fact, I get on pretty well with *most* women.

FRANCESCA: I think it must be—so beautiful to live with someone for ever. To stay and listen to them the whole time. To watch them eat their dinner and drink their coffee afterwards. And to tell them everything that's happened during the day —such lovely evenings together. One would be—so very *happy.*

ALBERTO (*during an acrobatic experiment in lighting a match*): Oh, I've thought of that, of course, too. People are bound to get married eventually, it's only natural.

FRANCESCA (*huskily*): Alberto. It's quite obvious what that girl Noemi is after. And Consalvo. 'Make up your mind', she said. 'Get things straight', etcetera. Don't you see?

ALBERTO (*finally lighting the match*): What? Do you mean . . .?

FRANCESCA: However you look at it, there's only one way of getting things straight so far as they're concerned.

ALBERTO: Oh, I don't really think so, you know.

FRANCESCA: Oh, yes, my dear.

ALBERTO: No, but think—you may be right about Consalvo; but what about Noemi? Good heavens, she laughs at all that sort of thing. She's sophisticated.

FRANCESCA: How simple you are, Alberto. She's a woman.

ALBERTO: But she's on my side. She's my ally.

FRANCESCA: But do you think she hasn't any secret thoughts of her own about you, deep down? If she hadn't she wouldn't have come rushing up here like this. I may be a country girl, but I have my eyes about me. Listen to me, Alberto. They'll both be back in a few moments. It's quite clear what they're after. If they don't find you here, what will they do? Run after you.

ALBERTO (*cheerfully*): Well, I'll run faster, that's all.

FRANCESCA: No, no, no. That's not the way. (*Embarrassment creeps into her voice*)

I'm quite sure that what you ought to do is to wait for them quite quietly here; and tell them—something definite—which will settle things once and for all—both for them and for us. (*She stammers*) Before *they* begin talking about marriage, don't you see, you ought to throw it in their teeth from the start. I am here—if you like I'll do it for you, gladly. You must shut them up at once; make them look silly. Like someone running to catch a train and finding it's already gone. Tell them it's useless to make so much fuss. Because you've already—made up your mind.

UGO BETTI *Summertime* translated by Henry Reed

Comprehension and Interpretation

1 Francesca's opening words mention the subject which is uppermost in her mind. To whom is she referring in the remainder of this speech?
2 Why does Francesca proceed to give a rosy picture of marriage?
3 Is there any indication that Alberto is not interested in marriage at that particular time?
4 Explain Francesca's remark: 'She's a woman.'
5 If you were acting the part of Alberto, how would you deliver the following line. 'But she's on my side. She's my ally.'
6 'No, no, no. That's not the way.' Why isn't this the course of action Francesca wants?
7 What is Francesca's opinion of Noemi and Consalvo? Which girl does she see as a rival?
8 Are Alberto and Francesca thinking about the same things in the first part of this extract? Write, in the form of a soliloquy, some of the thoughts which might have been passing through Francesca's mind whilst she is speaking.
9 List the points made by Francesca in her attempt to persuade Alberto.
10 Is it a good argument that Alberto should marry someone else in order not to marry Noemi or Consalvo? Give your reasons.
11 Write a brief character sketch of Alberto as he appears in his extract.

28

This is a typical American lookout tower where men and women fire-watchers are on twenty-four-hour duty to spot forest fires.

1 Imagine that you are one of these fire-watchers on an eight-hour duty. In this time you spot three forest fires, summon help and direct the fire-fighters to the exact position. A careful study of the tower will indicate the means of communication at your disposal.

At the completion of each hour of duty an entry, giving the following information, has to be made in the tower's logbook.

(*a*) Temperature.

(*b*) Weather conditions.

(*c*) Sightings other than fires, eg, people, cars, aircraft, etc. The time of sighting, the compass position and the distance from the tower, must be noted.

(*d*) Note time, position, and distance from tower, of all fires. Record action taken and the result.

Write the eight entries you would make in the logbook for your tour of duty. Commence each entry with the time and use the twenty-four-hour clock system.

2 Write a definition of a lookout tower. To do this you must first assign it to a general class and then show how it may be distinguished from the other things in the same class. For example, a lighthouse is a tower (general class), containing a beacon (first distinguishing feature) for warning ships at sea of danger (second distinguishing feature). You will note from the photograph that a lookout tower need not necessarily be a tower.

3 Describe in not more than 100 words the external appearance of this lookout tower.

29

Photographer Robin Adshead took this picture of a Harrier 'jump-jet' plunging to the ground after it had gone out of control. The aircraft crashed in flames but the pilot escaped with bruises and a broken ankle after parachuting to safety. He can be seen leaving the plane in an ejector seat powered by a rocket.

1 Supply a suitable title for this picture.
2 Write a sentence which expresses the motion of the aircraft on its downward path.
3 Give a definition of an ejector seat. Use a reference book if you need further information.
4 Try to imagine how it feels to be strapped to an ejector seat that is being thrust through the air by a rocket. Describe in a sentence or two the sensations of movement, noise and isolation.
5 Write a paragraph that describes the shape of the aircraft as seen in this picture.
6 Imagine the thoughts of the pilot in the moment captured by the camera. Write several sentences which express these thoughts.
7 The crash took place whilst the pilot was rehearsing for a Royal Air Force display in Cyprus. Write a description of the crash as seen by an observer on the ground.
8 This is the sort of accident which would be reported by the BBC. Summarise the crash in a paragraph for inclusion in a radio news bulletin.

30

Make a set of notes on the following passage. Supply suitable headings and sub-headings and give your finished notes a title.

Cotton is the world's most versatile fibre and has served mankind for at least 5,000 years. It accounts for over two-thirds of the total world consumption of all textile fibres.

Although the origin of cotton is obscure—the word cotton being derived from the medieval Arabic word 'Quttan' or 'Kutn', which means 'a plant found in conquered lands'—ancient records found in the Indus valley show that cotton was grown and used there as early as 3000 BC. Gradually the use of cotton spread throughout the Ancient World of the Far East and Near East and eventually was brought to European commerce by Italian merchant princes during the Middle Ages. Cotton manufacture was introduced into Britain by Protestant refugees from Holland towards the end of the sixteenth century.

During all these centuries the methods used were very primitive and were similar to those of the Ancient Egyptians who for thousands of years had spun and woven flax. But the principles employed were broadly the same as we use in these days of high-precision machinery and scientifically controlled production.

The cotton plant is one of the miracles of nature. It grows in warm subtropical lands where the climate and the soil are suitable. Each plant grows to between four and six feet and produces about a score of lovely flowers which live for only three days. Then the petals drop off and small green pods remain. These contain the new seeds—thirty or forty of them in each pod—and every one is attached to soft downy hairs like those in dandelion clocks. The pods keep swelling for about two months until they are as big as hens' eggs before bursting open to reveal the industry's raw material . . . cotton.

The ripe pod is known as the cotton boll. The cotton itself is just a tangled mass of fluffy fibres averaging about an inch in length. When picked—either by hand or mechanically—the bolls are poured into large machines called 'gins' which separate the fibres from the seeds and remove most of the stalk and bits of leaf. This is necessary because cotton in the raw state as it is picked from the field contains about half to two-thirds of its weight in seed, leaf, sand and other impurities which must be removed before it is suitable for delivery to the spinning mill.

Adapted from *Introducing Cotton*

31

Read the following poem carefully, and then:

(*a*) describe as vividly as you can the progress of the express through the countryside, and

(*b*) write a brief appreciation showing how the poet conveys an impression of power, speed and majesty.

The Express

After the first powerful, plain manifesto
The black statement of pistons, without more fuss
But gliding like a queen, she leaves the station.
Without bowing and with restrained unconcern
She passes the houses which humbly crowd outside
The gasworks, and at last the heavy page
Of death, printed by gravestones in the cemetery.
Beyond the town, there lies the open country
Where, gathering speed, she acquires mystery,
The luminous self-possession of ships on ocean.
It is now she begins to sing—at first quite low
Then loud, and at last with a jazzy madness—
The song of her whistle screaming at curves,
Of deafening tunnels, brakes, innumerable bolts.
And always light, aerial, underneath,
Retreats the elate metre of her wheels.
Steaming through metal landscape on her lines,
She plunges new eras of white happiness,
Where speed throws up strange shapes, broad curves
And parallels clean like trajectories from guns.
At last, further than Edinburgh or Rome,
Beyond the crest of the world, she reaches night
Where only a low stream-line brightness
of phosphorus on the tossing hills is light.
Ah, like a comet through flame, she moves entranced,
Wrapt in her music no bird song, no, nor bough
Breaking with honey buds, shall ever equal.

STEPHEN SPENDER from *Collected Poems* Faber & Faber Ltd.

32

Some of the results of the survey mentioned on page 10 are given in the following tables which the Editor has decided to publish. Study the tables very carefully and write the commentary required by the Editor to go with them.

1 Is Britain a Christian country?

	%
Britain is a Christian country	79·7
Britain is not a Christian country	19·0
Don't know/no answer	1·3

2 What is your religion?

	%
Church of England	63·4
Nonconformist	10·4
Roman Catholic	10·1
Presbyterian and Church of Scotland	8·9
Jewish	1·3
Atheist/Agnostic	1·1
Other religions	3·0
No religion	1·8

3 When did you last attend church?

	WITHIN 7 DAYS	WITHIN 3 MONTHS
	%	%
Church of England	6·2	24·1
Nonconformist	2·7	5·3
Roman Catholic	5·4	6·7
Presbyterian	1·6	4·1
Jewish	0·2	0·8
Atheist/Agnostic	—	0·1
Other religions	0·8	1·5
No religion	—	—

4 Should the present school religious arrangements continue?

AGE	21–24	25–34	35–44	45–54	55–64	65+
NO IN AGE GROUP	134	394	435	420	378	399
	%	%	%	%	%	%
Yes	86	87	91	93	88	92
No	11	11	8	6	10	6
DK	3	2	1	1	2	2

5 Should instruction be comparative or Christian only?

AGE	21–24	25–34	35–44	45–54	55–64	65+
NO. IN AGE GROUP	134	394	435	420	378	399
	%	%	%	%	%	%
Comparative	36	26	25	23	17	15
Christian	56	67	67	70	73	76
DK	8	7	8	7	10	9

33

Study the photograph carefully and then answer the following questions which are designed to test your observation and understanding.

1 Supply a suitable title.
2 Write a sentence or two explaining the facial expression of the girl.
3 Study the man's posture. How is he using his body?
4 How is the girl pulling herself up?
5 Write a paragraph describing the use of ropes in this picture.
6 If the girl were to slip where would the weight of her body be taken?
7 The man is dressed for climbing. List his outer clothing and in each case give a reason why it is being worn.
8 Give a brief description of the rock face.
9 Summarise the main idea of the photograph in one sentence.
10 Describe the chief features of rock climbing for someone who has never seen it before and who knows nothing about it.

34

Two Borstal Men on Run Caught by Lone A A Man

ALERTNESS OF AA MAN SAVES DRIVER

A A Man Fights Stack Fir

Patrolman swims to the rescue

AA MEN HELP PUT OUT LORRY BLAZE

AA man's heroism in car blaze

A A patrolman climbs 100ft., rescues woman

All of the headlines reproduced above refer to incidents involving an AA patrol. Select one of the headlines and write the story that lies behind it.

35

Read the following passage and then answer the questions below.

Forts of the Saxon Shore

Girdling the coast of south-eastern Britain, from Brancaster in Norfolk to Portchester in Hampshire, is a chain of mighty Roman forts. There were originally at least ten, possibly eleven, of which nine survive in varying states of preservation. They are generally known by the somewhat romantic name of 'Forts of the Saxon Shore' (*Litus Saxonicum*) and were commanded by an officer who bore the resounding title *Comes litoris Saxonici per Britanniam*—'Count of the Saxon Shore of Britain'.

Most were built towards the end of the third century A D, though some, eg. Richborough, incorporate portions of earlier buildings, and others, eg. Pevensey and Portchester, were adapted by the Norman and Plantagenet Kings and nobles and grew into medieval castles, while Reculver was built early in the third century and adapted for Saxon Shore Fort purposes. These four particular forts are now administered by the Ministry of Public Building and Works.

Let us look at the 'Saxon Shore' system as a whole. Here is a list giving their original Latin names and modern equivalents:

Branodunum/Brancaster
Gariannonum/Burgh Castle
Othona/Bradwell
Regulbium/Reculver
Rutupiae/Richborough
Dubris/Dover
Lemanis/Lympne
Anderida/Pevensey
Portus Adurni/Portchester

These are the nine forts listed in the *Notitia Dignitatum*, an official handbook of the civil and military organization of the Roman Empire which probably dates from between the fourth and fifth centuries A D. The identification of most of these forts is certain, but two are conjectural. Although nine forts are listed in the *Notitia*, we know from recent records that there was another Saxon-Shore-type fort at Walton Castle near Felixstowe; this might possibly have been *Portus Adurni* or *Othona*; it has since been swallowed up by the sea, so we may never know.

There are many Roman forts in Britain, especially in the North. Why then should these south-eastern strongholds excite attention? Because, although they vary somewhat in shape and size, they all have certain common characteristics. They are all on or near the sea, usually at strategic points—harbours or river-mouths—guarding the natural gateways which any seaborne invader of south-eastern Britain might attempt to force. Each could hold a substantial garrison, but it also adjoined a harbour from which a Roman fleet could operate. Few of the forts are on or near important Roman roads; communication between them must have been by sea.

Again, their general structure is broadly similar: high, heavy stone walls with projecting bastions for mounting *ballistae*—the Roman artillery; flanking ditches for additional defence; accommodation for a strong garrison with a naval arm. And they were built—or in some cases rebuilt—at about the same period, the latter part of the third century A D. Why?

The general assumption for many years has been that they were erected to act as protection against the Saxon sea-raiders who, at this period, were beginning to harry the coasts of Britain, Northern France and the Low Countries. There is in fact a parallel defensive system, a Gaulish *Litus Saxonicum*, on the other side of the Channel, from Mardyck, near Calais, southward as far as Blaye on the estuary of the Garonne (or alternatively Blavet in Brittany). It is exactly contemporaneous with the British 'Saxon Shore' defences and the names of the forts are also given in the *Notitia Dignitatum*. Again each of these forts, such as those near Rouen, Coutances, Avranches Vannes, Nantes, etc., was, like the British counterparts, on or near the sea-coast.

But there the parallel ends. The Gallic *Litus Saxonicum* does not appear to have been a closely knit defensive system, and whilst most of the forts were on or near the coast, five of them were *not* on navigable rivers or estuaries. Moreover each of these five stations guarded places well worth defending *in themselves*; they were not necessarily part of a general defensive system designed to prevent seaborne invaders penetrating into the hinterland.

LEONARD COTTRELL *The Roman Forts of the Saxon Shore*

Comprehension

1 What was the *Litus Saxonicum*?
2 Give the Latin title of its commander.

3 What was the Latin name of a Roman fort built early in the third century A D and later converted for use as a 'Fort of the Saxon Shore'?

4 What was the *Notitia Dignitatum*?

5 Most of the Roman forts can be identified but there is some doubt about two of them. Which are these?

6 Where was there another Saxon-Shore-type fort, not listed in the *Notitia*, and now under the sea?

7 List three characteristics which are common to the nine forts.

8 Name five structural similarities common to the 'Forts of the Saxon Shore'.

9 Give one reason why the forts were erected.

10 Where is there a similar defensive system, also listed in the *Notitia*, and built at approximately the same time?

11 List the essential differences between the two defensive systems.

12 Give reasons why you do or do not believe this passage to be a suitable one for comprehension.

36

It has often been said that a picture is worth a thousand words and photographs such as this have proved it.

In the photograph we have the port and holiday resort of Whitby in the North Riding of Yorkshire. A part of the town is shown rising steeply from the harbour until it meets moorland in the distance.

Study the picture with care and then summarise the information it contains.

Start by making rough notes about the harbour and the boats anchored in it. What are the boats used for and what do you deduce from this about Whitby as a port and holiday resort? Note also at this stage the activity along the wharf. Continue with the buildings around the harbour. Explain their layout in relation to the water front and then go on to assess their age, their use, and the materials from which they are constructed. End with notes on the streets and buildings of the remainder of the town. Try to obtain as much information as possible by a detailed examination of the photograph.

Expand your notes into a good, continuous prose summary of the picture.

37

1 Extract further information from this photograph to complete the following set of notes.

Log Unloader

I MOVEMENT

II CONTROLS

III LOAD

2 Write a factual description of this picture using the notes you have made as a basis for your work.

38

The following three items of mail were received by you during a week in May. Invent any further information you require and write a reply to each one. Consult a reference book if you have any doubts about the correct way to answer a formal invitation.

17, Rances Lane,
Woodstead,
Surrey.

22nd May

Dear......... ,

    I have seen your advertisement offering for sale a second-hand tape recorder. Would you be good enough to give me full details of the recorder and state the price you are asking?

        Yours faithfully,

James Collins

7, Seaview Road,
Bournemouth,
Hampshire.

24th May

Dear......... ,

    I am very sorry to learn about your mother's illness and hope she will recover quickly. Please give her my best wishes.

    Your parents intended that you should all spend your summer holiday with me this year, but I imagine that your father is too busy to think about it with your mother ill in bed. Would you please find out for me what arrangements they want to make and let me know shortly, as I have to consider other bookings for the rooms? In particular, please let me know what they want in the way of meals.

      I hope the rest of the family are well.

        Your loving aunt,

          Alice

Mr and Mrs T. J. Burford
request the honour of
your presence at the marriage
of their daughter
Margaret Kay
with
Mr Ronald James Hilton
at St John's Parish Church
Woodstead
on Monday, June 5th, at 11 a.m.
and afterwards at
the Imp Restaurant, Woodstead

16 Arnside Road
Woodstead
Surrey

R.S.V.P.

On the left, Mrs Sinclair's old dishwasher.
On the right, Mrs Sinclair's new Servis dishwasher.

For nigh on 12 years, Mrs Sinclair's dishwasher had performed perfectly.

Without so much as a murmur it would stand, bent over the sink, washing everything spotlessly clean.

Then, one day, the inevitable happened.

"This is insane" said the dishwasher. "Every day I wash up dozens of dishes. Not to mention knives and forks and pots and pans. In a year, it must run into thousands. Life's too short."

That, briefly, is why the Sinclairs decided to buy a dishwasher. Why they decided to buy a Servis dishwasher is another story altogether.

"It was the obvious choice really. My Servis washing machine these past ten years has been absolutely wonderful. Oh, there's been the odd thing now and again, but it's never really given any trouble.

However, quite apart from her faith in our products and our 700 strong team of after sales servicemen, Mrs Sinclair did find several other reasons for choosing a Servis dishwasher.

"It's big enough to take a whole day's washing up, so we usually only have to have it on in the evenings. And it takes all the pots and pans too. And you don't have to mess around rinsing things before you put them in or anything daft like that."

Finally, we asked Mr Sinclair if he didn't think it was a bit of a luxury owning a dishwasher.

"That's what everyone says" he replied. "But the way I look at it is this. No one thinks it's a luxury to have a washing machine. And you only use it once or twice a week.

A dishwasher you use every single day of your life."

Take a seat Mr Sinclair, you'll never have to wash up another dish again. Ever.

If it ever lets you down, we won't.
Servis

39

Make a careful study of the display advertisement reproduced on p. 76, read the information given below and answer the questions set.

Most display advertisements are a composition of picture, caption, copy, design and typography; all of which work together to produce a total appeal.

The Picture These are valuable in advertising because they conjure up a mood swiftly and are direct and quick in their appeal. This is needed in magazines and newspapers where the reader may be flipping over the pages with his mind on other things and has to be stopped long enough for the advertiser to get his message across.

The best pictures for display advertising are those that stop the reader by arousing his curiosity and induce him to read the copy to find out what is going on, or those that summarise the entire advertisement for the non-reader and telegraph the message whilst the page is being turned.

(*a*) Into which of the two categories mentioned above does this picture fall?

(*b*) Assess from the picture the income group and sex of the people it is aimed at.

(*c*) What message does the picture convey?

(*d*) What is it about the picture that is expected to appeal to us?

The Caption The caption is read by more people than the copy, and because of this the caption becomes a miniature advertisement to provide a message for those who read no further.

The caption in this advertisement offers a surprise comparison that stresses the advertiser's message and includes the brand name of the product. It also extends the appeal of the picture and offers a lead into the copy for those likely to read further. It is set in lower case because people are taught to read in lower case and find a sentence in capital letters much harder to assimilate. The caption may appear to be a long one but research has shown that long captions attract more readers than short ones.

The Copy This is set out in columns as most people acquire their reading habits from newspapers and are used to this method. The copy in this advertisement is lengthy but research has shown that lengthy copy containing information is more effective than brief copy without.

The opening paragraph is kept short as a long first paragraph tends to frighten readers. The remaining sentences and paragraphs in the first column are also kept short in order to tell a story in a conversational tone. The advertising message behind the story is that life is too short to spend time washing dishes by hand. The language extends the mood of the picture and the caption, and provides a smooth transition from the picture and the caption to that part of the copy in which facts are to be imparted.

Information about the product begins in the first paragraph of the second column where Mrs Sinclair gives her main reason for buying a Servis dishwasher. This item of information is repeated and enlarged upon by the advertiser in the paragraph that follows. The copy then reverts to a conversational tone in order that Mrs Sinclair may give further information about the product. The dialogue with the Sinclairs ends with the husband justifying the expense of buying a dishwasher.

The final paragraph returns to the mood of the picture and the caption, and the advertisement ends in bold type with another selling point and the name of the product.

(a) List the claims made for the product. Can they be checked?
(b) Write out the actual information given in the copy. How much of the copy is informational and how much persuasive?
(c) Consider the information given. What aspects of the product does this information stress? What aspects have been ignored? Write a short paragraph pointing out how the advertiser has used selected information.
(d) Does the copy remind you of any other sort of writing? If so, what?
(e) Which of the following forms of appeal is being made in the advertisement? To:
    (i)   sex
    (ii)   luxury
    (iii)   social status
    (iv)   dreams and fantasy
    (v)   men, women, or both
    (vi)   science and technology
    (vii) fear of non-conformity
    (viii) self-indulgence
    (ix)   sense of humour
(f) Assess the total appeal of the advertisement.

40

Read the following poem and then answer the questions on it.

Young Gazelle

Stiff as her Egyptian counterpart
Standing on legs of matchstick ivory,
She hides the racing of her heart,
While the black boss of her enormous eye
Flames inconsolable. Less like a deer
Than like a freckled girl, her skin's blanched gold
Drawn over little bones, her head held clear,
She listens, as if breathing were too bold.

A tremor, and she is still. Now sunny peace,
Light as the straw beneath her feet, persuades
Her pulses briefly. The terror goes—
Whipped by a childish whimsy of release,
She caracoles: a quick bound that evades
The bars. Then drops into a thrilled repose.

BABETTE DEUTSCH

1 Carefully explain in your own words the meaning of the following words as
each is used in its context in the above poem:
  (*a*) boss;
  (*b*) inconsolable;
  (*c*) whimsy;
  (*d*) caracoles.
2 What has the poet said in this poem?
3 Sum up the poet's attitude to the gazelle.
4 What effect did the poet intend this poem to have on the reader, and to what
extent has she been successful?
5 Explain the force of 'matchstick', 'blanched' and 'thrilled'.
6 Study the style of the poem. From the following list of adjectives choose *two*
which best describe the language used; pedantic, conversational, precise, elegant,
pompous, simple, strained, pretentious, humorous.

41

The aim of this section is to provide you with pictures on which to practise the close and accurate observation needed for good descriptive writing.

Take a quick look at the photograph of Fleet Street on page 80 and see what strikes you first about it. Make this impression the effect you will aim at in your description. Now study the photograph more closely and make accurate notes about the details. There will be too many to use in your description so be selective and choose only those which fit in with, or contrast with, the central theme you have chosen.

Most people first notice the objects in the photograph that are nearest to them and only afterwards do they become aware of the background and other details. This procedure can be followed as a pattern for your description or you can start from any other viewpoint so long as you group items together in paragraphs. It is important that you arrange your material and deal with one aspect of the scene before you go on to the next.

To make the description more imaginative it is essential that your reader feels that he is at the place you describe. To do this use words and expressions that appeal to the senses. Check over your notes and introduce where possible the colours, sounds, smells and movement that the photograph does not convey. Choose your adjectives with care and precision and avoid those which are over-worked and have therefore lost a precise meaning.

1 Use your rough notes to write a description under the title of 'Fleet Street'.
2 Write descriptions of the other two scenes using the method outlined above.

42

Answer any *two* of the following questions on your general reading.

1 Who is your favourite author? Mention the names of two or three of his books and explain carefully what it is about this writer's books that you particularly enjoy.

2 Choose three favourite villains from your reading. Do not tell the story of each book, but try to explain the character of each villain together with the reasons for your choice.

3 From the plays you have read select a part you would like to act in a film, play or broadcast. Discuss fully how you would portray the part, how you would walk and talk, the sound of your voice, what you would wear and the effect you would hope to have on your audience.

4 You have been asked to present a twenty-minute programme of poetry readings for a radio broadcast intended for people of your own age. Your selection should be based upon a theme. Detail your selection and say briefly why each item has been included.

5 Dramatists can amuse their audiences by creating comic characters and by creating amusing situations. Give examples of both of these and then describe fully a scene from a play which has amused you.

6 Give an appreciation of any poem you have studied. Start with a brief summary and then go on to the form of the poem and its appeal. Give your views on the success or otherwise of the poem, whether or not you like it and the reasons for your views.

43

Reduce this passage to note form by following the method outlined on page 222.

Amber is not a mineral, but a fossilized resin or gum. It was formed millions of years ago in the Oligocene Age when certain types of coniferous trees grew in abundance, died, and were buried in the earth. The land sank under the sea, and in the blue clay which formed, amber is found—sometimes with flies or other insects embedded in it. It is light in weight, warm to the touch, and, unlike resin, does not become sticky when rubbed. The colour of amber ranges from white to darkish brown, and there are also reds and bluish and greenish tints. It may be transparent or cloudy.

From earliest times amber has been used for necklaces and amulets, and there are many superstitions and legends connected with it. Some of these undoubtedly owe their origin to its power, when rubbed, of attracting small pieces of paper. The ancient Greeks called it *elektron*, and it is from this that we get our own word electricity. In addition to its use as a charm, amber was once thought valuable as a medicine. Worn as a necklace it was supposed to cure ague and prevent goitre; ground up into a paste with honey a dose would help deafness or a salve improve eyesight! The early Chinese burned it as incense.

Some of the earliest-known roads in the world are those by which amber from the Baltic was taken overland to the more civilized people of the Mediterranean. These are dated as early as 2000 BC in the early Bronze Age, and much earlier than this the Baltic peoples of the New Stone Age were using it in quantity and burying it in their graves. Today the most important source of amber is still the Baltic coastlands of Germany and the USSR, though small supplies come from Sicily, southern England, Roumania, and Burma.

As amber is brittle and breaks easily, great care has to be taken in working it; but when carved and polished it is very effective and has for long been used for jewellery and delicately carved ornaments.

Oxford Junior Encyclopaedia, Vol. III, p. 12

44

1 Below are printed some diagrams relative to weekly service magazines for women. Study them carefully, make notes on the main facts and any inferences to be drawn from them, and then write as much as you can on the information you have gathered.

Net circulation in millions of copies

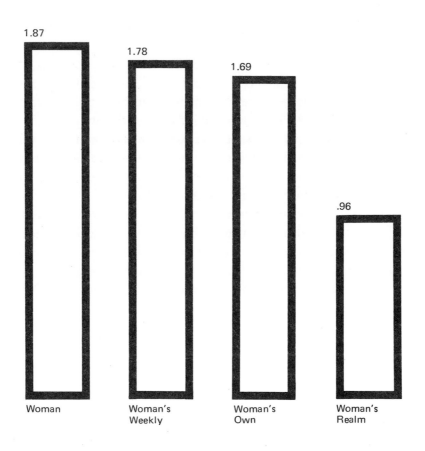

Woman	Woman's Weekly	Woman's Own	Woman's Realm

Source: ABC July–December 1973

Readers of one or more woman's service weeklies *

By Age

15 to 24   54%

25 to 34   52%

35 to 44   52%

45 and over   49%

By Social Class

upper and middle   54%

lower middle   52%

working and poor   46%

total   51%

* Woman, Woman's Own, Woman's Realm, Woman's Weekly

2 Make a careful study of the editorial content analysis given below. Obtain copies of the service weeklies mentioned and check the contents against the items listed. At the same time make notes on your reactions to the various features and articles. Use the material you gather to write an article on the content of women's service weeklies.

Editorial Content Analysis

	Woman	Woman's Own	Woman's Realm	Woman's Weekly
	%	%	%	%
Personal Features				
The Family				
Fiction				
Total	42	44	42	46
Human relationships	4	6	3	2
Attitudes to life/religion	1	1	1	4
Horoscopes and the occult	2	2	1	1
Fiction	19	20	22	33
Fashion	5	4	5	1
Beauty	6	8	5	3
Family Wellbeing	5	3	5	2
Practical Features				
The Home				
Total	22	21	32	34
Home planning	4	2	6	1
Gardening and house-plants	*	1	*	2
Food and Wine	7	7	14	8
Handicrafts	11	11	12	23
The Outside World				
Total	32	30	22	16
Features	19	16	8	9
Information	7	5	4	1
Offers	4	6	7	6
Reader's Service	2	3	3	*
Miscellaneous				
Total	4	5	4	4
Grand Total	100	100	100	100

*Less than 0.5%   *Source:* IPC Magazines Ltd

45

Read the following extract and then answer the questions that follow it.

Lawrence Persuades the Sheik

AUDA (*passionately*): El Aurans, I have no great love for the Turks. Feisal is my friend and I would be his ally. But what are you asking? A march in the worst month of the year across the worst desert in Arabia—el Houl—the desolate—that even the jackals and vultures fear—where the sun can beat a man to madness and where day or night a wind of such scorching dryness can blow that a man's skin is stripped from his body. It is a terrible desert—el Houl—and terrible is not a word that comes lightly to the lips of Auda Abu Tayi.

LAWRENCE (*mildly*): I had believed it a word unknown to him.

AUDA: My friend, your flattery will not make wells. And it will not stop the few wells there *are* on the fringe of that desert from being poisoned by the Turks the moment they learn of our objective—as they must—

LAWRENCE: Why must they?

AUDA: Do you think I am unknown in Arabia? Do you think that when Auda rides out at the head of five hundred men the Turks will not ask questions?

LAWRENCE: Indeed they will, but will they get the right answer?

AUDA: They are not fools.

LAWRENCE: No. And that is why the last thing they will look for is an attack across el Houl on the port of Akaba. If such a project seems mad even to Auda, how will it seem to the Turks?

AUDA (*chuckling*): By heaven—there is some wisdom there, el Aurans. They would not even guess at it. No sane man ever could—

LAWRENCE (*taking the map*): But just in case they do, the direction of our march should be north-west at first, to make them believe we are aiming at a raid on the railway.

AUDA (*abstractedly interrupting*): Has Feisal much gold?

LAWRENCE: Alas—he is rich only in promises—and so am I on his behalf.

AUDA: And what would you have promised me if I had consented to this madness?

LAWRENCE: A higher price than the Turks would pay.

AUDA: Then it must be high indeed. What is it?

LAWRENCE: The praise of the whole world for the most brilliant feat of arms in Arabian history.

Pause

AUDA (*gazing at the map*): Akaba! Even your own all-powerful Navy has not dared to attack it.

LAWRENCE: Oh yes.

AUDA: And were defeated?

LAWRENCE: Oh no. Our Navy is never defeated.

AUDA: Well?

LAWRENCE: After a successful bombardment they withdrew.

AUDA: Beaten off by the Turkish guns.

LAWRENCE: They are very powerful guns.

AUDA: Have I powerful guns?

LAWRENCE: You have no need of guns.

AUDA: How? No need?

LAWRENCE: There is no gun—however powerful—that can fire backwards.

Pause.

AUDA: They all point out to sea?

LAWRENCE: All out to sea.

AUDA: Fixed?

LAWRENCE: Fixed.

Pause.

AUDA: How strong are the Turks?

LAWRENCE: About two thousand in the area.

AUDA: Against five hundred?

LAWRENCE: Four to one. Auda's odds.

AUDA (*chuckling*): Auda's odds. Have they made no preparations against an attack from the land?

LAWRENCE: None.

AUDA: They believe it impossible?

LAWRENCE: A madman's dream.

AUDA (*chuckling*): The fools. No fortifications facing the land at all?

LAWRENCE: A few—a very few—but they will be easy to surprise.

AUDA: A camel charge, at night. My battle cry, to panic the idiots from their beds, and then amongst them.

LAWRENCE: They may well surrender at the very sound.

AUDA (*genuinely alarmed*): May Allah forbid! My friend, do you think I am marching across el Houl in the deadliest month of the year, to be rewarded at the end with a tame surrender?

LAWRENCE: Well—then—perhaps no battle cry—

AUDA: That, too, is unthinkable. Even Turks must know who it is that kills them. A charge in daylight, then—after due warning—

LAWRENCE: Not too long a warning.

AUDA: Not too long and not too short. Akaba! What a gift to make to Feisal—

TERENCE RATTIGAN *Ross*

Comprehension

1 List the seven reasons given by Auda for not crossing the el Houl desert.
2 Why does Lawrence think that the Turks will not expect an attack on Akaba from the direction of the desert?
3 What payment is Auda to receive for helping Lawrence to capture Akaba?
4 Why is there to be a march to the north-west before the desert crossing begins?
5 Name the method of transport to be used in crossing the desert.
6 Write a brief, accurate description of the defences of Akaba.
7 What are Auda's reasons for deciding that his men will charge on Akaba in daylight?

Composition

Imagine that you made the journey across el Houl with Lawrence and Auda and took part in the attack on Akaba. Write a vivid description of *one* of the following:

(*a*) A day's journey, without water, on the final stage of the crossing of el Houl.

(*b*) The charge on Akaba.

46

The use of stale language is one of the hardest faults in writing to eliminate because it saves the writer the trouble of thinking how to express effectively what he wants to say. A casual glance at the photograph on p. 92 will bring to mind, almost automatically, several phrases which have been used over and over again to describe a fire in a shop.

tongues of flame
night sky ablaze with light
windows silhouetted against the flames
gutted interior
skeleton of a building
hoses snaking across the road

It is difficult to avoid the use of clichés like this, especially if one does not know they are clichés. Some English textbooks provide lists of clichés to memorise and avoid, but a better method is to study what you see until you have in your own words what most accurately describes it.

1 Concentrate upon the fire in the photograph. What is it like? Does it remind you of anything else? Try to find a comparison which is based upon keen observation and the result of your own thinking. Do not make too wide a gulf between what you see and what you are reminded of as this will lead to bizarre comparisons. Make a list of your comparisons in freshly coined language.

2 Study the remainder of the photograph and make similar lists for
   (*a*) the building;
   (*b*) the road;
   (*c*) the firemen.

3 Write an original description of this picture using the best of the images coined by you for Questions 1 and 2.

4 Write a short, factual account of the fire in plain, straightforward language. Give the main details of the incident—when, where and how it happened, how long it lasted, the Fire Brigade called, whether people were involved, and so on.

47

Study the following photographs of the RSW Compact bicycle and then answer the questions below.

1 Give reasons why you like or dislike the appearance of the bicycle.
2 How has the use of the bicycle affected its design?
3 Supply a definition of a bicycle.
4 Write a factual description of the RSW Compact in not more than 200 words.
5 List five good selling points for a publicity leaflet.
6 Imagine that each of these photographs is to be used in display advertisements. Write advertising copy to accompany each photograph.
7 Think of another everyday object whose design has changed radically during recent years and describe how it differs from the traditional design.

48

Read the following passage and then answer the questions set on it.

Pot

Pot, Indian hemp, Cannabis Indica, reefers, kif, marijuana, mahjnoun—what do the names make us feel? Probably something dark and desperate, an evil habit, brought here by dissolute black men from somewhere we'd sooner not know about, the kind of thing our children are bound to take to if we don't have them inside and locked up by ten o'clock. If they do they will surely become degraded, unrecognisable, tragic wrecks, sexually depraved, thin, with burning eyes, exploited by gangsters and criminal entrepreneurs, paying more for their necessary doses, etc., etc. Our laws reflect all this; cannabis is covered by the dangerous drugs legislation, those who deal in it are imprisoned amid toots of obloquy, and the stuff fetches magnificently high prices.

The whole thing is one of the most mysterious bits of our *mores*. Pot is not a habit-forming drug at all; the last inter-departmental committee set up to inquire into drug addiction, reporting in a White Paper in 1961, stated quite flatly that 'cannabis is not in our opinion a drug of addiction'. It did not waste further words on it, but continued its discussion of the large number of drugs in common use as tranquillisers and pain-killers which are. It also committed itself to the view that addiction to alcohol was a serious problem in Britain, and seemed to regret it was outside its terms of reference.

It would indeed be difficult to devise a study which would yield valid figures about this, but I guess that if you introduce a hundred adolescents to liquor (who would not otherwise have met it) you make one alcoholic: if you introduce them to pot you make one pot-addict: if you introduce them to tobacco—cigarettes, you make five lung-cancer deaths, if you introduce them to heroin you make eighty junkies.

Pot is not habit forming, it is not even a *drug*, in the sense that cocaine and heroin and morphine and the barbiturates are. It is, as the White Paper said, an intoxicant, like alcohol. It increases both happiness and depression, according to which was present when it was taken. A tremendous lot gives rise to rather pleasant disturbances (though hardly hallucinations) in the visual sense; things look brighter, like Van Gogh, more sharp-edged, like Botticelli, more important. It is something to be taken at parties as drinks are. There is no joy in taking it alone, and nobody does. All in all, it feels like a variant of alcohol. It is not aphrodisiac; it doesn't seem to deaden the inhibition mechanisms in the way alcohol does. Nor does it make for vomiting or 'stupor'. You have to smoke lots of reefers in quick succession to feel anything much: to compare it with alcohol, one reefer is perhaps rather less than half a pint of beer. It can produce a hangover, though, just as alcohol can.

In some parts of the world, notably North Africa, it is socially equivalent to our use of alcohol. People smoke it, or eat it in spoonfuls of jam, after meals, and above all at parties. They feel about mahjnoun, as they call it (marijuana is the Spanish form of this Arabic word) as we feel about alcohol, and they feel about alcohol as we feel about marijuana. They fear and despise alcohol; it is prohibited to Muslims by the Koran.

Naturally, after the French occupation, and during the strenuous puritanism of their own nationalist revolutions, mahjnoun is getting a bad name, but that is an infection from European attitudes and does nothing to prove they are justified.

Now we surely have enough things in life to make us miserable without inventing more. I don't know how we first came to fear cannabis; it seems as though some mistake was made.

Perhaps it arose during the times when we feared everything about people who were darker-skinned than us. We feared their religion, their politics, their geography, their art forms (steel bands were actually *prohibited* in Trinidad until after the Second World War, when at last an unsquare governor went out and danced in the street) and so why not their intoxicants, too? The fear of cannabis goes with the feeling that brown and black people are dirty sexy beasts, and that sitting on the floor and eating with one's fingers is disgusting, instead of just different. The tragi-comedy is that our simple little mistake led us to bracket pot with the really dangerous drugs, heroin, cocaine, etc., against which all possible sanctions are justified. It may prove hard to disentangle it, but the attempt ought to be made quite soon.

If it is not, the trouble will not so much be that we deprive ourselves of an innocent pleasure; we have alcohol, which is just as good. The trouble is that many people are deeply distressed if they hear of the spreading of this habit, and their distress is unnecessary. For one thing, it introduces a needless strain between the races and between the generations. A reform of the law would do something to remove this strain. A possible way to go about it would be to permit the growth, processing, importation, and sale of hemp and reefers on the same footing as alcohol; taxed and regulated alike.

It is not deadly, like tobacco, and might be a good alternative source of revenue.

WAYLAND YOUNG from an article in *The Guardian*

A Comprehension

1 Why does the writer begin the article with 'Pot, Indian hemp, Cannabis Indica, reefers, kif, marijuana, mahjnoun . . .'?
2 The inter-departmental committee studying drug addiction stated that 'cannabis is not in our opinion a drug of addiction'. List three searching questions you might ask the committee before you would be prepared to accept such an opinion.
3 Does the writer think that reefers are more harmful than cigarettes or less harmful?
4 How reliable is the information given in the third paragraph?
5 Consult a good dictionary and then in your own words write a definition of the word 'drug'. Name four of the habit-forming drugs mentioned in the article.
6 Tabulate, in two columns, the advantages and disadvantages of taking pot.
7 What are the differences between Muslims and ourselves so far as marijuana and alcohol are concerned?
8 What suggestion does the writer make to account for our fear of Indian hemp?
9 Study the following extracts from the passage and then write a sentence or two arguing that cannabis *is* a drug of addiction, and a serious problem.
   (a) 'It also committed itself to the view that addiction to alcohol was a serious problem in Britain, and seemed to regret it was outside its terms of reference.'
   (b) '. . . if you introduce a hundred adolescents to liquor (who would not otherwise have met it) you make one alcoholic: if you introduce them to pot you make one pot-addict. . . .'
10 Summarise the main idea of the article in one sentence.

B Comprehension and Composition

Read Wayland Young's article again with the intention of criticising the argument it contains. Pay particular attention to the following:

(i) the lack of supporting medical evidence;

(ii) the contradictions;

(iii) the suggestion that as reefers are like alcohol they should be permitted because the consumption of alcohol offers few dangers;

(iv) the sentences in the article which begin with such words as 'Perhaps', 'I don't know', 'Probably', and 'It would indeed be difficult'.

Now study the following extracts and use the information, along with any other facts you are able to obtain, to write a 500-word article in which you expose the weaknesses in Wayland Young's argument and attack his point of view on marijuana and alcohol.

'**Marijuana (Marihuana)**. Marijuana, an intoxicating excitant drug used illegally in the United States and elsewhere usually in cigarette form, is obtained from the top leaves and flowers of the Indian hemp plant, *Cannabis sativa*, which grows in most parts of the world. Since ancient times people have used its products for stimulation and intoxication. Abusive use of it is a serious medical and social problem in various countries. Many emotionally unstable persons known to be associated with major crimes prove to be marijuana users. Marijuana intoxication may be accompanied by such physical and psychic manifestations as thirst, hunger, craving for sweet foods, nausea, dizziness, abdominal pain, drowsiness, irritability, delusions of grandeur or persecution, uncontrollable hilarity, talkativeness, apprehension, mental confusion, prostration, depression, inarticulate speech and delirium. Mental dullness ordinarily increases with continued use of marijuana and psychoses may develop. Some persons have suffered most disagreeable effects a short time after smoking one marijuana cigarette.

Withdrawal of marijuana causes no such physical abstinence symptoms as opiate withdrawal does. Addiction to heroin or morphine commonly follows use of marijuana, especially among young persons.

Marijuana, considered to have no medical value, was removed from the United States pharmacopoeia. The federal Marijuana Tax Act of 1937 prohibited its use. It was placed under international control because of its increased abuse throughout the world. The World Health Organisation undertook a project to develop a strain of the hemp plant devoid of intoxicating resins.'

Encyclopaedia Britannica

Phases in Alcoholism

Stage of Excessive Drinking

More time spent in social drinking
Drinks more nights of the week
Sneaks drinks
Takes stronger drinks than companions
Adopts strategies to get more drinks
Preoccupied with drinking
Drinks to get relief from tension
Increased tolerance
Guilt over drinking
Social failures excused to himself and to others with fabricated explanations
Needs drink to perform adequately at work or socially
Feels drink has become a necessity
Increased guilt feelings

Stage of Alcoholic Addiction

Onset of alcoholic amnesias (memory losses)
Greater frequency of amnesias
Loss of control—compulsive drinking
Reduction in interests
Drop in work efficiency
Absenteeism
Drunk in the daytime
Reproof from employer or relatives
Low self-esteem
Remorse
Compensatory bragging and generosity
Financial extravagance
Deceives family, debts made
Increasing social isolation
Aggressive outbursts
Wife takes over more responsibilities
Deterioration in relation with wife
Paranoid misinterpretations

Self-pity
Justifies drinking with self-deceptions
Reduction of sexual drive
Morbid jealousy
Drunk at weekends
Loss of job
Breakup of family
Morning tremulousness
Morning drinking
Conceals supplies of liquor
Repeated attempts to stop drinking
Suicidal impulses and attempts
Neglects meals

Stage of Chronic Alcoholism

Physical and mental symptoms dominate
Loss of appetite, poor food intake
Continuous drinking
Tolerance diminishes
Prolonged confused thinking
Use of cheap wines and methylated spirits
Delirium tremens
Goes to Alcoholics Anonymous or seeks medical treatment
Serious physical diseases

NEIL KESSEL AND HENRY WALTON *Alcoholism*

49

This photograph shows a combined Saturn 5 rocket and Apollo spacecraft before launching.

Saturn 5 is 281 feet tall and has three stages. The first is 138 feet tall, 33 feet wide, and has five rockets clustered at its base. The second stage sits on the shoulders of the first, is 82 feet tall, and also 33 feet wide. The third stage is nearly 59 feet tall but tapers off to just over 21 feet in width.

The Apollo spacecraft perches on top of Saturn 5 and has a launch escape tower above it. With spacecraft and launch tower installed the total height is 363 feet.

1 Use the following plan to write a good description of Saturn 5 and its spacecraft. Make use of the photograph and the information given by selecting from each what you require to complete the description.

Plan

(a) Definition.

(b) Use.

(c) Mainparts.

(d) Approximate size of parts.

(e) Colours—so far as can be ascertained.

(f) Shape of the whole—refer to shapes of numbers, letters of alphabet or geometrical figures.

2 Write two paragraphs explaining the use of the ground support equipment shown on the left of the rocket.

50

Make a careful study of both the plan and the photograph of Pevensey Castle. Assemble notes from the plan, the photograph, the information given and the passage for comprehension on page 67. Arrange the notes in the best order and then write them up into a factual description of the castle.

Pevensey Castle, Sussex

Origin	late third century A D.
Walls	stone, horizontally bonded with red brick, twelve feet thick, projecting bastions.
Area	ten acres.
Shape	irregular oval.
Function	Saxon Shore Fort, site later used by Normans who built a castle within the walls.

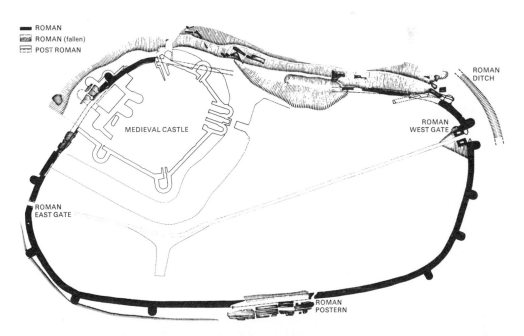

ROMAN
ROMAN (fallen)
POST ROMAN

ROMAN DITCH

ROMAN WEST GATE

MEDIEVAL CASTLE

ROMAN EAST GATE

ROMAN POSTERN

51

Turn to page 227 and revise the section dealing with the interpretation of statistics. Study the following tables, which deal with the growth rate of some of the world's cities, and then write a short article conveying the information you have gathered.

The World's Biggest Cities   (population in millions)

	1970	1985	Growth rate %
New York	16.3	18.8	15
Tokyo	14.9	25.2	69
London	10.5	11.1	6
Shanghai	10.0	14.3	43
Paris	8.4	10.9	30
Los Angeles	8.4	13.7	63
Buenos Aires	8.4	11.7	39
Osaka	7.6	11.8	55
Moscow	7.1	8.0	13
Peking	7.0	12.0	71
Calcutta	6.9	12.1	75
Rio de Janeiro	6.8	11.4	68

The World's Fastest Growing Cities   (population in millions)

	1970	1985	Growth rate %
Bandung	1.2	4.1	242
Lagos	1.4	4.0	186
Karachi	3.5	9.2	163
Bogota	2.6	6.4	146
Baghdad	2.0	4.9	145
Bangkok	3.0	7.1	137
Teheran	3.4	7.9	132
Seoul	4.6	10.3	124
Lima	2.8	6.2	121
Sao Paulo	7.8	16.8	115
Mexico City	8.4	17.9	113
Bombay	5.8	12.1	109

52

1 Write a letter of application suitable for the post advertised below.
2 Write two testimonials to support your application.

PAGES

Slough Maidenhead Windsor

Applications are invited from boys and girls about to complete their
GCE O Level Examinations for

STUDENTSHIPS

in one of Pages Department Stores

Retailing offers an interesting, progressive, satisfying career for a boy or
a girl with good personal qualities, a liking for people and reasonable
academic ability. A student receives systematic instruction in the various
branches of retailing with continued education on a day release basis.

Full wages are paid during the studentship and there are excellent staff
amenities and conditions including a five day week.

**Written applications should be sent to the
Director of Personnel
Pages Ltd
Slough
Buckinghamshire**

53

Selection of words and material is important if you are to be an effective writer. It is possible to produce two very different pieces of writing on the same topic if you select some points and omit others, and your selection can be used legitimately or to persuade and deceive. This extract from a typical holiday brochure will illustrate the technique.

Flor de Mar

A tumbling rock coast, broken by shimmering blue bays, ringed by perfect beaches, and set against a background of pine-clad hills which verge on broom and heather. No wonder they call Flor de Mar the jewel of the Costa Brava! Flor is the most enchanting holiday spot in the whole of Spain. Postcards make it look great, but it is even better in the flesh!

One of the three charming beaches sweeps for two miles along the full length of the town, and the gleaming, white sand is as soft as wheat flour. The rocky inlets provide wonderful bathing and there is fabulous swimming in the world's warmest, bluest, truest sea. Bathe, sunbathe—or just lie around whilst you are served with drinks and refreshments from bars on the beach. And always the sun is shining from a blue, blue sky.

For those of a more athletic nature there are pedalos (water cycles) for hire, tennis, sailing, and so on, whilst sea fishing trips can be arranged with the sturdy local fishermen. It is a wonderful coast for underwater fishing or just plain under-water gazing, and the beautiful grottoes and caves nearby are just asking to be explored.

When the evening sun goes down it is the sign for all heaven to cut loose. Shower and change, admire your sun-tanned body in the mirror, sink a leisurely aperitivo, and then step out for the night's fun. The fascinating cafés and bars have real Spanish dancing; wild, authentic flamenco and fandango accompanied by throbbing guitar-playing and singing. These nights of beautiful people, music, wine and laughter, mixed with the heady, exotic perfume wafting from the carnation plantations, will fill your mind with enchanting memories to be treasured for years.

One unforgettable feature of Flor is the intriguing Sardana, the local dance in which the warm-hearted inhabitants love strangers to join. The music is played on a local pipe called a flabiol, whilst the dancers, hand in hand, man and woman alternately, dance in circles. When the ring gets too large another one is formed and the simple, graceful dance goes on.

You'll love the old, medieval town surrounded by its immense, fourteenth-century towers and walls. The genuine Crusaders' Castle seems untouched by time and as you explore it the pages of history are turned slowly back. In the town everything is shade and elegance, with cool squares and cafés, carafes and clinking glasses. The shops are really something—full of smart things and all at fantastically low prices. Flor has long attracted artists from all over Europe and the town has a small, but very fine, art gallery for the art lover.

From Flor you can make many delightful coach and boat excursions along the Costa Brava. Trips to wondrous Barcelona, gayest and largest city in Spain, provide an exciting contrast. You can be there in an hour and spend the day among some of the most exciting and glamorous shops in the world. Sip your sherry at a café table and watch people from every country in Europe pass by, or join the colourful crowd to watch the vivid, ritualistic drama of a bullfight. And then back to *your* town by nightfall.

Flor is like a gigantic bouquet offered just for you. Take it in a holiday that you will never forget.

In this description of Flor de Mar the words and material have been selected to show it as an attractive holiday resort. Note that the beaches are 'perfect' and 'charming', the sand is 'gleaming white' and 'soft as wheat flour', the bathing is 'wonderful' and 'fabulous', the inhabitants are 'warm-hearted', and everything in the town is 'shade and elegance'. Our common sense tells us that every holiday resort has some drawbacks, but no mention is made of this side of the truth. Anything which is detrimental to the image of a holiday paradise has been left out.

Another aspect of this description is its use of emotive language, ie, language which appeals to the emotions through words and word-pictures and triggers-off other associations. The fourth paragraph, for example, contains such phrases as 'admire your sun-tanned body in the mirror', 'nights of beautiful people, music, wine and laughter', and 'fill your mind with enchanting memories to be treasured for years'.

Study the passage again and make sure you understand the technique involved and then answer the following questions.

1 Make notes on the passage to show the plain, basic facts about Flor de Mar.
2 Use a similar selective and emotive technique to write a description which will attract visitors to your own area or your favourite sea-side resort. Without

actually lying, make everything sound as attractive as possible, even those things a visitor would not normally be interested in.

3 You have been staying at Flor de Mar for the past ten days. Use your imagination to write a letter to a friend and in it reveal what the place is really like.

4 Write a description, using a selective approach, to portray your own locality in the worst possible light. Omit the favourable and stress the unfavourable.

5 Write a second description of your locality and this time concentrate on the facts so that a balanced picture of the area emerges.

54

The figures given below are the result of a by-election held in a town where the electorate numbered 65,000

	votes	%
Conservative	18,280	53.1
Labour	9,892	28.7
Liberal	6,232	18.2
Total	34,404	

In a General Election held one year earlier the result had been:

	votes	%
Conservative	25,610	52.4
Labour	15,109	30.8
Liberal	8,213	16.8
Total	48,932	

Study both sets of figures carefully and then answer the questions below.

1 Write a description of what happened in this by-election without quoting any of the figures given.

2 Explain in about 100 words how the by-election result differed from that of the General Election.

3 Write two news items, complete with headlines, in which you report this by-election for (a) a Labour newspaper, and (b) a Conservative newspaper. Remember to compare the result with that of the General Election and bear in mind that the electorate numbered 65,000.

55

The excerpts that follow were taken from the written work of American college students who were asked to express their views of the world and their roles in life. Read the excerpts with care and then summarise the outlook of this group of young people.

(*a*) 'I want to accomplish something in my life that will make the world a better place. I want to help bring about peace and brotherhood and make joy the prevailing emotion.'

(*b*) 'The thing that is of greatest concern to me in world affairs is peace, not because I fear death through conflict, but because the absence of peace means the presence of unhappiness. I wish that everyone in this world could have enough of three things—food, good health, and love. As an individual I will never be able to supply enough food for the peoples of the world, nor will I be able to discover a secret formula for continuous good health. But I do have the ability to provide a little more love, pleasure, and happiness.'

(*c*) 'I am concerned with racial equality and I am angered by and cannot understand prejudice. I would like to take up sociology to further my understanding of this problem and perhaps contribute something to its solution.'

(*d*) 'I am an individual who wishes to remain one. I do not feel the world owes me anything, rather that I must leave the world a better place for my being, and that I must fight for what I believe and believe what is right and true at any cost. . . . I love people and would like to contribute something to the world in which I live. Some possibilities which interest me are teaching and social work.'

(*e*) 'The things that are most important to me are those instances that are most immediately and directly related to the understanding and improvement of relations and communications between people. . . . My most basic desire is simply to be very aware of what is going on today and to try my hardest to understand what is happening.'

(*f*) 'Love, happiness, using all of my resources and talents and developing them to the best of my ability, are very important to me. They are important because they are the first step for me to take in becoming a successful, first-class citizen.'

(*g*) 'I don't expect to become rich. Money doesn't interest me that much. But, if by chance I do come into some money, I'm not going to burn it. Money does have its place. All I want is for people to help people. . . . But money isn't enough; people have to care. That's one thing that I think is important, caring.'

(*b*) 'I don't specifically know what it is that I want to do. It will probably involve work with children in what the social workers call "underprivileged areas". I want to do something that matters, changes and improves.'

Quoted by DR R. S. PITKIN *Young America*

56

Make a careful study of the four photographs of Chichester Festival Theatre and extract information in note form.

Arrange the notes in logical order and write them up in good, plain English to give a clear explanation of the interior and exterior of the theatre.

116

57

A hoarding carries a number of advertisements and in each one a different method of appeal to the passer-by has been used. Study the following quotations from the advertisements and for each one explain, in a sentence or two, how the advertiser makes his appeal.

(a) Firelight, soft music, romance—and, of course, Black Velvet Chocolates.

(b) If you are one of those people who insist on the best . . . . .

(c) Drink Black Diamond—the man's beer.

(d) Any Marlow's Biscuits, Mum?

(e) Does your skin hide a secret?

(f) Cumberland Tobacco—a few pence more per ounce, but so worth it.

(g) Sooth away the cares of her day. Give her a night of peaceful sleep with an evening cup of Nightcap.

(h) Caiger's Old Fashioned Mints. Unchanged since Granny was a girl.

The following quotations were also taken from the hoarding. Write a sentence or two criticising each one.

(a) Laboratory tests prove that 20% fewer cavities occur with Pearl Toothpaste.

(b) Girls are attracted to men who look fit!

(c) Alkaset relieves indigestion twice as fast.

(d) Beer is Best.

(e) Asprates are twenty times more effective than aspirin alone. Nothing works faster than Asprate.

(f) The secrets of the Tutor whisky blend have been guarded for the past 150 years.

The characters in the advertisements on the hoarding included the following:

a pipe-smoking, tweedy countryman;
two men in white laboratory coats;
a harassed housewife;
a beer-drinking boxer.

Give reasons why each of the above characters were chosen by the advertiser. Find examples of other advertising characters and analyse their function in the advertisements.

Composition

Tell the story of John Howard, a man whose whole way of life has been moulded by advertisements.

58

This is an expressive photograph. Note the wreath, the dejected attitude of the man, and the bare, gloomy passage.

Write a short story which uses the situation in the photograph as its final paragraph. Start with a happy incident (this will make a contrast between the beginning and the end) and arrange the subsequent incidents in a logical order so that they lead to the final situation. Try to make every sentence and paragraph add something to the development of the story.

59

This Lambretta scooter caught fire after its electrical equipment had short-circuited. Study the picture with care and then answer the questions which follow.

1 It is unlikely that you have seen a photograph like this before. Explain why it is unusual.
2 Give three reasons that lead you to believe that this photograph was not taken in Britain.
3 Describe, from the evidence in the picture, what action the owner took to extinguish the fire.
4 Write a paragraph expressing the *motion* of the flames.
5 Study the posture of the male onlooker in the background. What does his attitude suggest?
6 What do you think would have been different about this picture if the incident had taken place in Britain?
7 Write a factual account for your local newspaper of a scooter that caught fire. Supply the name and address of the owner, state whether or not he was injured, give the name of the road and the town in which the incident occurred, the time of day and the date, and the action taken by the police and firemen.

60

You are the secretary of Holgate Youth Club and you receive this letter after some of your members have been on a Youth Hostelling expedition.

Write a tactful reply to the Warden accepting responsibility for the damage and suggesting a possible arrangement of reparation.

GREENLAWNS HOSTEL

Heckton Hamlet, Parkstone, Barsetshire. Tel: 025 586 326 Registered number:983938

```
The Secretary,
Holgate Youth Club,
Holgate,
Surrey.                              21st August
```

Dear Secretary,

          The room occupied by your party last week was given a routine check after your departure and it was found to be damaged.

          Apart from surface scratches to the floor and chairs it was also discovered that one of the beds had two of its supports broken. A quotation from a local carpenter has placed the cost of repair at £15, and until this is carried out the bed cannot be used.

          Your Club was given permisssion to use the Hostel on the understanding that it accepted responsibility for any damage caused, and I therefore await your comments.

                 Yours faithfully,

J. C. Simmonds

                 Warden

61

Collect five different newspapers of the same date and then carry out the following assignments.

1 Write short reports on each of the following:

 (a) the five front-page headlines;

 (b) the five editorials;

 (c) the treatment of five identical news items.

2 Analyse any two of the newspapers and make a note of:

 (a) three news items in each that do not appear in the other;

 (b) one news report that corresponds in every important respect with the report in the other;

 (c) three facts or figures which differ significantly in each;

 (d) two news items appearing in both papers in which description is used to colour your impression of the event;

 (e) two examples of comment or opinion that contradict each other about the same event.

 Write paragraphs which account for any three of the above.

3 Use the five newspapers to obtain the essential news and then compose a radio news bulletin for that evening.

4 Make a careful study of any gossip column in any newspaper. Write a parody of the column basing your news items on gossip among your friends.

5 Readers' letters are a popular feature of most newspapers. Write three short letters typical of those appearing in:

 (a) the *Daily Mirror* and the *Sun*;

 (b) the *Daily Express* and the *Daily Mail*;

 (c) *The Times*, *The Guardian* and *The Daily Telegraph*

6 Choose a newspaper with which you are familiar and describe the character of a typical reader.

7 You wish to launch a new daily newspaper because you are not satisfied with the present ones. Explain how the new paper would be different.

8 Newspapers give us a mixture of news, general information, views and entertainment. Examine your own interest in a particular paper; which parts of it you read and why you read them. Write a short report on your newspaper reading habits.

62

One way to make your writing more interesting is to notice the similarities between people, actions, objects, buildings, etc., even when the similarities are not at first apparent. This will not only make your writing more satisfying, it will also give you more to write about. If the habit is developed it may produce some unusual and significant ideas.

The differences between these two photographs are obvious. Forget them and search for the similarities that do not appear at first glance. Note the follow-my-leader attitude of the cattle and the fact that they are in a pen. Is there anything similar to this in the other photograph?

This assignment requires a great deal of preliminary study and thought because it is not an easy one. In particular, Question 3 may prove difficult unless you give both pictures very careful consideration.

1 Write out two popular sayings in which people are likened to cattle.
2 List five similarities between the students and the cattle. You may use the suggestion already made.
3 Think of a single idea or common denominator for the two photographs. Organise your thoughts and observations to show that each picture is a variation of your idea. Write a comparison of the two photographs using your idea as a thread running through it.
4 Describe the similarities between young girls watching their favourite popular star giving a performance on the stage and spectators at a football match.
5 Compare your best friend with a person you actively dislike and then describe the similarities between them.

63

Imagine that you are staying with friends in London and that one evening they take you to a Spanish restaurant for a meal. Use this photograph as a basis for an imaginative description of the evening.

The picture will provide you with details of the restaurant, its customers, furnishings and general atmosphere. If you lack knowledge of Spanish food then visit a library to make notes on the type of Spanish dishes which might be served.

The girls are performing a flamenco dance in traditional costume and further notes will be necessary to make this part of your description authentic. The photograph will give you information about the dancers' dress, ornaments, arm movements and the musical background to the dance.

Ensure that your description is a vivid one by introducing the colours, sounds and smells which the photograph does not convey.

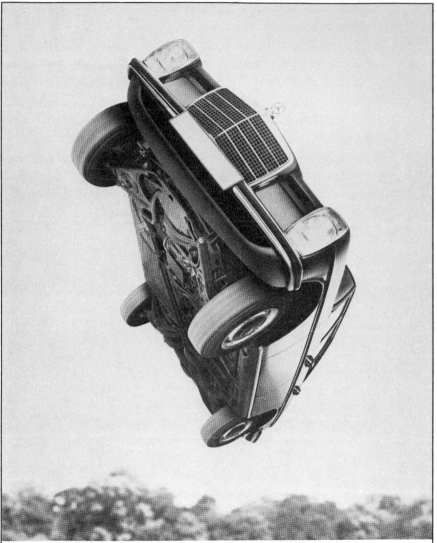

No one ever achieved greatness without making a few sacrifices.

If you think about car safety a good deal these days, it's hardly surprising.

The idea that cars should be safe as well as speedy is finally catching on. In the press. On T.V. On the radio. Everywhere.

It wasn't always so. Ten years ago, the public at large wasn't at all safety-conscious. For an advertisement to talk about luxury cars crashing would have been unthinkable.

But to say that no one was talking about safety is not to say that no one was doing anything about it.

At Mercedes-Benz, as you probably know, we've been crash-testing cars for many years, putting hundreds upon hundreds of Mercedes through roll-over tests, head-on tests, side-on tests. And why?

Because although we patented the world's first car safety body way back in 1951, it was to take another eight years' work before it was ready for series production. And another fourteen years after that to bring that original 'safety cell' up to the even higher standards it has reached today.

Safety isn't an overnight job, something you can suddenly decide to build into next year's models. To produce cars that can fairly be called safer demands an enormous outlay of money, talent and time.

We plough back a higher percentage of our turnover into research and development than any other car manufacturer in the world. If it only ever saves one life, it's cheap at the price.

Mercedes-Benz

The Mercedes-Benz range includes Saloons, Sports Saloons, Coupés and Limousines. Prices from £3,689 to £17,950.
Mercedes-Benz (Great Britain) Ltd., Great West Road, Brentford, Middlesex TW8 9AH. Telephone 01 560 2151. A member of the Thomas Tilling Group.

64

Make a careful study of the advertisement reproduced on page 128 and then answer the following questions. A revision of the exercise on page 77 may be helpful.

1 Explain the point of the picture.
2 Comment on the effectiveness of:
   (*a*) the caption;
   (*b*) the copy;
   (*c*) the layout.
3 To whom is this advertisement directed?
4 Assess the appeal of the advertisement and comment on the devices used in making it.
5 Find three other examples of display advertisements and make a critical analysis of the techniques used.

65

Use the following information as a basis for a composition of about 350–500 words on the subject of 'Folk-Music'. Gather any further material you may need and follow the plan for writing given on page 218.

1 There are three main types of folk-music,

(*a*) dance and work song, probably the oldest type;

(*b*) legendary folk-song, also of early origin;

(*c*) composed folk-song, more recent.

2 Folk-music in the past was music which grew up among people as part of their work and leisure. Each generation handed folk-music to the next and until recent years it was never written down.

3 Great political movements have been responsible for folk-songs, eg, the slavery of Negroes in the USA and the subsequent freedom movement.

4 Composers have incorporated folk-music in their works, eg, Tchaikovsky and *Ouverture Solennelle—The Year 1812*. Themes from folk-music also appear in jazz and popular music.

5 Folk-music is played on such instruments as the guitar, castanets, banjo, bagpipe and tambourine.

6 Folk-song differs from country to country, eg, British and American folk-song generally tells a story. Folk-song from warmer climates is usually louder and more vigorous.

7 Some examples of folk-song are:

Streets of Laredo	The Foggy Dew	Careless Love
We Shall Overcome	The Old Grey Goose	Barbara Allen

Additional exercises

1 Choose any modern folk-song you like and explain what emotions and thoughts it expresses, and what the song means to you.

2 Why has modern folk-song a particular appeal to young people? Quote from the lyrics of several folk-songs to support your answer.

3 Select a folk-song that appeals to you and compare it with one of the usual hit parade songs. Comment on the performers, the lyrics and the musical arrangements to show why one is superior to the other.

66

Read the following and then answer the questions set.

An Uneasy Relationship

This extract is taken from *The Night of the Iguana* by Tennessee Williams.

Shannon is a highly strung ex-priest who is reduced to escorting sightseers around Mexico on third-rate tours. He is constantly in trouble with his tourists and finally one of them telephones back to Texas and Shannon is officially sacked. This starts a brainstorm; he becomes violent and has to be tied down on a hammock on the hotel veranda.

Hannah is a spinster who travels with her aged grandfather and earns money by selling drawings.

In this scene Shannon is tied to the hammock and is talking to Hannah. Neither of them can be of permanent help to the other, but both recognise each other's loneliness and agony of mind.

(*Now all have left but Hannah and Shannon.*)

SHANNON: Untie me.

HANNAH: Not yet.

SHANNON: I can't stand being tied up.

HANNAH: You'll have to stand it a while.

SHANNON: It makes me panicky.

HANNAH: I know.

SHANNON: A man can die of panic.

HANNAH: Not if he enjoys it as much as you, Mr Shannon.

(*She goes into her cubicle directly behind his hammock. The cubicle is lighted and we see her removing a small teapot and a tin of tea from her suitcase on the cot, then a little alcohol burner. She comes back out with these articles.*)

SHANNON: What did you mean by that insulting remark?

HANNAH: What remark, Mr Shannon?

SHANNON: That I enjoy it.

HANNAH: Oh . . . that.

SHANNON: Yes. That.

HANNAH: That wasn't meant as an insult, just an observation. I don't judge people; I draw them. That's all I do, just draw them, but in order to draw them I have to observe them, don't I?

SHANNON: And you've observed, you think you've observed, that I like being tied in this hammock, trussed up in it like a hog being hauled off to the slaughterhouse, Miss Jelkes.

HANNAH: Who wouldn't like to suffer and atone for the sins of himself and the world if it could be done in a hammock with ropes instead of nails, on a hill that's so much lovelier than Golgotha, the Place of the Skull, Mr Shannon? There's something almost voluptuous in the way that you twist and groan in that hammock —no nails, no blood, no death. Isn't that a comparatively comfortable, almost voluptuous kind of crucifixion to suffer for the guilt of the world, Mr Shannon?

(*She strikes a match to light the alcohol burner. A pure blue jet of flame springs up to cast a flickering, rather unearthly glow on their section of the veranda. The glow is delicately refracted by the subtle, faded colours of her robe—a robe given to her by a Kabuki actor who posed for her in Japan.*)

SHANNON: Why have you turned against me all of a sudden, when I need you the most?

HANNAH: I haven't turned against you at all, Mr Shannon. I'm just attempting to give you a character sketch of yourself, in words instead of pastel crayons or charcoal.

SHANNON: You're certainly suddenly very sure of some New English spinsterish attitudes that I didn't know you had in you. I thought that you were an *emancipated* Puritan, Miss Jelkes.

HANNAH: Who is . . . ever . . . completely?

SHANNON: I thought you were sexless, but you've suddenly turned into a woman. Know how I know that? Because you, not me—not me—are taking pleasure in my tied-up condition. All women, whether they face it or not, want to see a man in a tied-up situation. They work at it all their lives, to get a man in a tied-up situation. Their lives are fulfilled, they're satisfied at last, when they get a man, or as many men as they can, in the tied-up situation. (*Hannah leaves the alcohol burner and teapot and moves to the railing, where she grips a veranda post and draws a few deep breaths.*) You don't like this observation of you? The shoe's too tight for comfort when it's on your own foot, Miss Jelkes? Some deep breaths again—feeling panic?

HANNAH (*recovering and returning to the burner*): I'd like to untie you right now, but let me wait till you've passed through your present disturbance. You're still indulging yourself in your . . . your Passion Play performance. I can't help observing this self-indulgence in you.

Comprehension and Interpretation

1 What is Shannon's argument for being untied and how does Hannah react to it?
2 Why does Shannon feel insulted by Hannah's remark?
3 What is the difference between observing people and judging them?
4 Quote the phrase spoken by Shannon which indicates that he feels Hannah's observation may be wrong.
5 What evidence is there that Hannah understands Shannon's wish to suffer for his sins and those of others?
6 In Hannah's view, what is the essential difference between Shannon's self-indulgent mental crucifixion and the physical crucifixion of Jesus Christ?
7 Think carefully about the idea of mental crucifixion. Which can be the more painful, mental or physical crucifixion?
8 List the remarks made by Shannon which indicate that Hannah's cool character sketch of his condition is not providing the sympathetic treatment he is looking for.
9 'All women, whether they face it or not, want to see a man in a tied-up situation.' Mention two situations which might fit Shannon's remark. Do you agree or disagree with this statement? Give your reasons.
10 'The shoe's too tight for comfort when it's on your own foot, Miss Jelkes?' Explain this remark.
11 Quote the stage direction which indicates that Hannah feels there is some truth in Shannon's comments about women.
12 One of the functions of a passage set for comprehension is that it should stimulate and challenge us to think afresh about ourselves and the world around us. Give your reasons why you do or do not believe that this passage has made you think afresh about people and their relationships with others.

67

The pictures in this section have been chosen to enable you to write from a particular viewpoint.

Take each picture in turn, identify yourself with any person in it, and project yourself into the situation shown. Get definite ideas about the time of day and year, the people you are with, the atmosphere, your character and personality, your home background, and your way of life.

Write your observations about each of the four situations from the point of view of the character you imagine yourself to be.

68

Read the following passage and then answer the questions that follow it.

A Chinese Meal

A table set for a Chinese meal is a most inviting sight. Merely to look at it seems to stimulate the anticipatory juices that are so important. At each place is a plate, two porcelain bowls—one larger than the other, two porcelain spoons with short handles like medicine-spoons, a pair of ivory chopsticks and two small round dishes. One of these contains mustard sauce and oyster sauce and the other usually soya-bean sauce. There is a paper napkin beside each plate and beside every other chair an enamelware spittoon for the gentlemen. All this inviting array looks very sad when the feast is at last over, because it is not considered to be particularly bad manners to make a mess on the tablecloth. That is what tablecloths are for. The result is that when the guests rise from their places in two and a half hours' time the table looks indeed as though an orgy had taken place. As a matter of fact the Chinese spill their food about very little, but Europeans, who are less skilled, do. When I have finished, the floor around my chair is usually covered with spilt rice as though snow had been falling.

The other guests on this occasion were one European, a Government servant, some Chinese business-men, a lawyer, and their wives. They came round the screen and we bowed as we were introduced. Then we sat down as directed by our host cheek by jowl, or rather hip to hip and thigh pressed against thigh, on little metal chairs around the enticingly laid-out table. As usual the meal began with little bowls of jasmine tea, delicious and fragrant, and damp hot cloths were handed round on a tray from which they were proffered to us with tongs. On these we wiped our hands and the men their faces, but not the ladies for fear of spoiling their make-up. In the good old days, whenever those were, these cloths were soaked in rose-water, but in these degenerate times it seems to be nearly always disinfectant. Then the meal began. A sort of *hors d'œuvre* came first, tiny cockles from northern China in their shells, minute fragile birds, which could have been larks, eaten whole, and slivers of 'abalone', which is the *Haliotis* shell. After that I cannot recall the sequence of dishes, but I remember that at first I looked up in eager anticipation as each one arrived. As a rule there are as many courses as there are diners, so that presently my eagerness turned to misgiving, and then to dread, and finally to despair. Sweat burst out on my forehead. I felt I was beginning to swell visibly and began furtively undoing buttons. I have learnt better now and know that you must hold your horses and attack the first few dishes lightly. Even if you take only a few mouthfuls from each dish you are sure to have eaten more than enough before the end comes. The succession is in the opposite order to that of a European meal, beginning with chicken, duck or meat, or all three and sometimes more than one dish of each, followed by fish (several perhaps) and then soup. Lichees or sliced oranges or baked apples dipped in syrup usually bring the meal to a merciful end. Everything, needless to say, is of celestial deliciousness. The Chinese are perhaps the most skilled cooks in the world, and all their various cuisines are the products of centuries of trial and error and perhaps also the products of centuries of famine and shortage when all sorts of things had to be eaten and made palatable. The Chinese indeed, eat practically anything, birds' nests, sharks' fins, toads, frogs, lizards, all cunningly disguised to please fastidious tastes. Behind the scenes in any Chinese restaurant, no matter how smart its external appearance, is a spectacle of inferno-like squalor, where celestial foods are nonchalantly prepared, amid clamour and steam and shouting and clatter, angry sizzlings and licking tongues of flame. Out of these infernal regions there were borne into us, and set down steaming before us, sucking-pigs of which one ate only the crackling, ducks which seemed to have fallen asleep with their bills beneath their wings while being cooked, but which fell apart at a touch and were stuffed with lotus seeds. There were fledgling pigeons which were eaten whole, skull, beak, skeleton soft as jelly, entrails and all. There was chicken with walnuts and carp cooked in ginger, rice and bamboo shoots and sharks'-fin soup, which has the same indefinable satisfying quality that oysters have. Finally there were apple slices cooked in syrup. You dipped them in cold water so that the syrup turned to toffee. It is impolite to pass over any of these delicacies even if one's eyes are not, as mine are, larger than one's interior. So that it was really with unspeakable relief (I could scarcely speak by now in any case) that we at last greeted the arrival of a dish of sliced oranges, which really meant the end.

We drank Chinese rice-wine, or *shau shing*, which is served warm and is rather like a volatile sherry, rich and giggle-inducing. After the meal we drank a fiery liqueur also made from rice. It traced its course in neon lights down to the midriff, where it stayed and glowed like a small coal.

F. D. OMMANNEY *Eastern Windows*

Comprehension and Note-making

1 Compile six questions of your own which are designed to test whether a reader has understood this passage.

2 Exchange your questions with a friend and answer the questions he has compiled.

3 You are the host who is responsible for this meal and a servant is to lay the table for you. Make out a list for him of the china, napkins, etc., which will be needed by the twelve diners. Give the exact number required for each item you list.

4 The author says that he cannot recall the sequence of the dishes, but he does give the order of the courses and a list of the food eaten. From this make out a menu card for the meal using the following headings—hors d'œuvres, meat, fish, vegetables, soup and dessert. Do not forget the sauces, wines and tea.

69

1 Write a full paragraph describing the atmosphere captured in this picture.
2 Imagine that you are the girl in the bikini. Give your views on beachwear.
3 Why are the three critics wearing coats, hats and scarves, and carrying umbrellas and handbags? In this respect how does their mental attitude differ from that of the girl?
4 Bikinis are classed as swimwear but are not considered suitable for Olympic swimmers and serious swimming. Why are they worn?
5 Provide a suitable title for the photograph.
6 Write a conversation in play form between Ena, Martha and Minnie on the subject of bikinis and the modern girl. Imagine that the conversation is part of a TV script and that it takes place in Ena's home after the holiday is over.

70

This photograph was published in a national newspaper and it shows a sculptor, Mr Mateer Fisher, with his fibre-glass figure of Paul McCartney. Unfortunately, Mr Fisher has portrayed Paul as a right-handed guitar player when in fact he is left-handed.

Write a letter to the Editor of the newspaper pointing out the sculptor's mistake and expressing your opinion of the fibre-glass figure. Use the name and address of the newspaper you normally read and invent any other information you require.

71

Read the following poem carefully, than answer the questions on it.

Chough

Desolate that cry as though world were unworthy.
See now, rounding the headland, a forlorn hopeless bird,
trembling black wings fingering the blowy air,
dainty and ghostly, careless of the scattering salt.

This is the cave-dweller that flies like a butterfly,
buffeted by daws, almost extinct, who has chosen,
so gentle a bird, to live on furious coasts.

Here where sea whistles in funnels, and slaps the back
of burly granite slabs, and hisses over holes,
in bellowing hollows that shelter the female seal
the Cornish chough wavers over the waves.

By lion rocks, rocks like the heads of queens,
sailing with ragged plumes upturned, into the wind
goes delicate indifferent the doomed bird.

REX WARNER

1 Sum up the writer's attitude to the chough as expressed in this poem.
2 Comment on the poet's use of metaphor and onomatopoeia.
3 Use reference books as a basis for notes on the Cornish chough.
4 Explain the force of 'fingering' and 'wavers'.
5 Which three words from the poem would provide the most suitable alternative title?
6 Write a short description of the seascape as visualised by the poet.

72

Make a survey of the record sleeves at home and those in the window of the nearest radio or music shop. Use this information, together with that given below, to write an article of 500 words or more on the subject of 'Record Sleeves'.

1 The record sleeve is a remarkable symbol of modern photographic packaging.
2 Music is now bought with the eyes.
3 For years records were sold in plain sleeves, but today it would be impossible to sell a long playing record, however good, in a plain sleeve.
4 The photograph, and the colour photograph in particular, has come to dominate the display windows of radio and music shops.
5 Records are often given as presents and the sleeve plays an important part as a gay packaging.
6 Imagination is the source of music and imagination is the source of the record sleeve.
7 A relationship between music and photography has been discovered and music can now be interpreted photographically.
8 The musical content of a sleeve is often shown as follows:

(a) classical music has abstract designs, architecture, and cultural or antique motifs;
(b) the works of Bach carry pictures of seventeenth-century objects such as furniture, musical instruments and interiors of houses;
(c) folk-dances feature romantic landscapes or people in folk-costume;
(d) symphonies are depicted by a wide range of pictures ranging from the play of waves to 'still-life';
(e) light and dance music is contained in bright, daring, racy sleeves;
(f) photographs of artists enjoying current popularity appear on sleeves containing their works.

73

A Premium Bond given to you as a birthday present won a prize of £1,000. You invested £700 and used the remainder to pay for a holiday for yourself and your best friend. You decided to go to Dubrovnik in Yugoslavia and stay at the Hotel Argentina. This hotel is situated on the seashore, has its own beach, an indoor and outdoor swimming pool, and a tennis court.

Write at some length an imaginative account of the fifteen days you spend at Dubrovnik. Use the information given below and if necessary supplement it with any you obtain from the library or nearest travel agency.

Holidays in Yugoslavia

Climate The climate on the Adriatic coast is Mediterranean. The coast is famous for its sunshine and Dubrovnik has an average of 2,630 sunny hours per year.

Currency. The monetary unit is the dinar and the following banknotes are used: 5, 10, 50, 100 and 500 dinars. There are also coins of 5, 10, 20 and 50 paras, and 1, 2 and 5 dinars. Travellers can take unlimited amounts of foreign currency into Yugoslavia in cash, cheques and travellers' cheques. Currency can be exchanged at authorised banks, and exchange offices in travel agencies, trains, hotels and some post offices.

Food Breakfast is usually Continental: rolls and butter with jam and tea or coffee. Lunch and dinner are substantial and mostly Yugoslav. You'll eat a lot of meat—veal, pork and lamb—and plenty of greens and salads. The food is rich so don't overdo it at first. The local specialities include Adriatic fish dishes, *bosanski lonac* (cabbage, cheese, eggs and spinach), *musaka* (egg-plant with minced meat) and *sarma* (minced meat and rice in sauerkraut or vine leaves).

Drink Coffee is usually served by the pot with breakfast and dinner. A stimulating variation is the black, Turkish coffee served in a little brass jug and drunk in a small cup. It is hot, sweet and strong. Yugoslav tea is refreshing but does not match its English equivalent. Beer is either draught or bottled, light or dark. The dark variety is sweetish. Bottled light beer is the most readily available, has a lager taste and is served ice-cold. Yugoslavia is well known for her vineyards and has many excellent wines and spirits. Red wines include *prokupac*, *vranac* and *plavac* whilse *traminac*, *silvanac* and *riesling* are good white wines. A famous national drink is *silvovitza*, plum brandy, mostly sold at 60 proof, but watch out for the heady 90 proof.

Beachwear Temperatures have a high summer average, so take lightweight clothes. Bikinis may be worn and minimum beachwear is usual. In some more casual resorts beachwear is worn from dawn to dusk.

Shopping Shops are open on Saturdays until 3 pm As a rule, shops work in two shifts: from 8 am to 12 am, and from 4 pm to 8 pm However, many shops, especially general stores and self-service shops, are open throughout the day, and some are also open on Sunday mornings.

Souvenirs Any quantity of souvenirs may be taken out of the country on the condition that they have been bought with imported foreign currency. In all the larger towns and tourist resorts there are *Narodna Radinost* (Folk Crafts) shops where one can buy such articles as hand-made embroidery, lace, leather goods, woodcarvings, silver filigree jewellery, hand-made rugs, national costumes and ceramics.

Entertainment Most of the cities have theatres and there are cinemas everywhere (some of them open-air) with British and American films with Yugoslav subtitles. Folk-dancing in national costume is a colourful and exciting spectacle and may be seen from time-to-time. There is dancing in the evening in the larger hotels and especially the lively open-air cafes.

Medical facilities Yugoslavia has a National Health system similar to our own. An agreement exists whereby visitors from the United Kingdom can receive medical attention under the Yugoslav public health service should the need arise.

Language Most hotel staff speak and understand English, but a knowledge of German and Italian is useful as they are most widely understood.

Flying time to Dubrovnik Airport

From Gatwick Airport by Boeing 707	2 hrs 25 mins
From London Airport by Boeing 707	2 hrs 65 mins
From Birmingham Airport by TU-134A	3 hrs
From Manchester Airport by Boeing 707	3 hrs
From Glasgow Airport by DC-9	3 hrs 20 mins

Baggage allowance 15 kg (33 lbs) from Birmingham and Glasgow, 20 kg (44 lbs) from Gatwick, London and Manchester.

74

Read the following passage carefully and then make a summary of it in not more than 200 words. You are advised to revise the information given on page 220 of the Reference Section before you begin.

With no thought of this in her head, only the need pressing on her to have the lock empty and the gates open by the time her boats drew into sight, Nanette slopped her way all round the lock, down one side, across the sloping slippery beams of the shut gates and up the other side to close the other gate. Enormously heavy, it yet swung in the full water lightly to and fro, played upon by every ripple, as loose and easy as an unanchored dinghy. Nanette gave it a last angry push to settle the matter and trotted back to wind the opposite paddles.

Afterwards she leaned over, watching the smooth face of water that lay outside at the foot of the gates. A blossom, a moving flower, broke through the surface like a lily thrusting upwards to unfold, silently and hurriedly, its petals. Another dawned, and then another, and then the water was heaved up in violent confusion and tossed and torn aside by a great escaping flurry, a torrent, a noisy avalanche of white and green. It tumbled and poured out from the open sluices, and at the far end the gates banged heavily together as the level in the lock sank and the water was sucked from them.

Nanette stretched herself at full length along a beam and lay there at her leisure, rain on her face and the odour of old soaking wood in her nostrils. She turned her cheek and found close to her eye a world, enlarged to immensity, of small green mosses, chips and pebbles, a weed or two, stranded and living together in a cleft of the wood with the tranquillity of ignored existence.

The rush of water slackened; she sat up. The lock was almost empty. Outside, the tumult had ceased and only brownish froth and large shining bubbles floated away in breaking, dissolving circles. At the same moment her ear caught the familiar pattering, and round the corner appeared the bows of the *Venus*. Rather gingerly, for this was one of the things she hated and feared to do, she slithered her feet down to the point where the two great gates met one another. Standing on one of them and holding very firmly indeed to the hand-rail, she began with her left foot to press the other gate apart and push it wide open. It moved grandly a few inches, she shoved again desperately, stretching her legs wide, clutching with all her terror to safety. Terrible visions of the slip, the fall, and death by drowning beset her as she poised there, straddled between the two gates, one of them reluctantly moving from her. She kept her foot upon it as long as she dared, encouraged it with a last backward kick, and retreated thankfully to the lockside to push open the second gate. The alternative way of opening gates was to run all round the lock again, and as the day was full of locks and running, a little danger and fright was preferable to greater fatigue.

EMMA SMITH *Maidens' Trip*

75

Read this passage carefully and then answer the questions that follow.

Money spent on advertising is money spent as well as any I know of. It serves directly to assist a rapid distribution of goods at reasonable prices, thereby establishing a firm home market and so making it possible to provide for export at competitive prices. By drawing attention to new ideas it helps enormously to raise standards of living. By helping to increase demand it ensures an increased need for labour, and is therefore an effective buttress against unemployment. It subsidises many services: without advertisements your daily newspaper would cost four times as much the price of your television licence would need to be doubled, and travel by 'bus or tube would cost 20 per cent more.

And perhaps most important of all, advertising provides a guarantee of reasonable value in the products and services you buy. Apart from the fact that twenty-seven Acts of Parliament govern the terms of advertising, no regular advertiser dare promote a product that fails to live up to the promise of his advertisements. He might fool some people for a little while through misleading advertising. He will not do so for long, for mercifully the public has the good sense to refrain from buying the shoddy article more than once. If you see an article consistently advertised, it is the surest proof I know that the article does what is claimed for it, and that it represents good value.

Advertising does more for the material benefit of the community than any other force I can think of.

There is one more point I feel I ought to touch on. Recently I heard a well-known television personality declare that he was against advertising because it persuades rather than informs. This is hair-splitting with a vengeance. Of course advertising seeks to persuade.

If its message were confined merely to information—and that in itself would be difficult if not impossible to achieve, for even a detail such as the choice of a typeface is subtly persuasive—advertising would be so boring that no one would pay any attention. But perhaps that is what the well-known television personality wants.

I am prepared to make just one concession to the opponents of advertising. Not every advertisement is a good one. Nor, for that matter is every parson. But if a bishop has toothache, is the whole Church sick? Some advertisements are vulgar. (So are lots of people.) Some are boorish. Some are silly. Some are pointless. Not very many. Pick up the nearest magazine or newspaper and count the advertisements that really offend you. And then count the advertisements that, in some degree, interest you or give you pleasure. And be honest!

T. E. JOHNSON *One Off*

Note-making

1 You have been asked to speak in favour of advertising at the next meeting of your school discussion group. Read the passage carefully and make notes for the speech you will give.

2 What are the arguments against advertising which might be put forward by the opposition? List as many of these as you can.

76

This piece of sculpture by Ezio Martinelli is mounted on the east wall of the General Assembly building at United Nations Headquarters in New York. It is an abstract design in gold and bronze-coloured anodised aluminium and measures 30 by 17 feet.

Study the work carefully and then answer the following questions.

1 Write a clear, factual description of the sculpture in plain, straightforward English. You may incorporate the information given.

2 Martinelli has said that this sculpture does not represent or symbolise anything in particular and that each viewer must interpret it in his own way. Make an imaginative study of the work and note ideas as they occur to you. It may help to ask yourself the following questions:

(*a*) Does the whole work, or part of it, remind me of something else I have seen? For example, a crown of thorns, a jungle of TV aerials.

(*b*) Does it suggest another image? An idea? Something out of this world?

(*c*) Is it a distorted representation of a familiar emblem?

(*d*) Does it convey a feeling of unrest, harmony, aggressiveness, etc?

(*e*) What is it not?

When you have finished your study, write a short but imaginative account of the sculpture. The aim here is not to supply a description as in Question 1, but to record what imaginative pictures the work has suggested to you.

3 Summarise your impressions and provide the sculpture with a short title.

4 A friend looking at the photograph remarks that this sort of modern sculpture is rubbish and has no value. He adds that a child of ten could do better. If you agree with him write an account attacking Martinelli's work; if you disagree then write a defence of it.

The following table was compiled by the Road Injuries Research Group of Birmingham Accident Hospital and shows the types of injuries received by 500 people killed in road accidents. Study the table carefully and then state in the form of a written report the conclusions you have drawn.

CATEGORY OF ROAD USERS	PEDESTRIANS	RIDERS OF MOTOR-CYCLES SCOOTERS OR MOPEDS	PEDAL-CYCLISTS	VEHICLE OCCUPANTS	TOTAL INJURIES
Fractures					
Spine	38	18	3	8	67
Legs	99	26	6	16	147
Arms	42	19	2	15	78
Pelvis	77	14	2	11	104
Ribs, Sternum, Clavicle	89	41	20	59	209
Skull, Face	134	73	32	75	314
Major Soft-tissue injuries					
Brain	161	77	36	85	359
Cord	14	9	1	8	32
Kidneys, Adrenals	14	12	5	5	36
Lungs	70	36	15	57	178
Liver	20	20	6	25	71
Spleen	14	19	4	18	55
Stomach, Bowel	15	10	3	4	32
Bladder, Urethra	13	4	3	3	23
Diaphragm	—	2	—	1	3
Major Blood-vessels	24	24	5	22	75
Total Injuries	824	404	143	412	1,783
Complications					
Severe Blood Loss	112	52	15	58	237
Pulmonary Embolism	15	—	—	7	22
Fat and Air Embolism	8	1	—	3	12
Infection	30	5	3	6	44
Deaths	231	102	45	122	500

Read carefully the following passage, and then answer the questions set on it.

The Rain-Horse

It would be quicker to go straight forward to the farm a mile away in the valley and behind which the road looped. But the thought of meeting the farmer—to be embarrassingly remembered or shouted at as a trespasser—deterred him. He saw the rain pulling up out of the distance, dragging its grey broken columns, smudging the trees and the farms.

A wave of anger went over him: anger against himself for blundering into this mud-trap and anger against the land that made him feel so outcast, so old and stiff and stupid. He wanted nothing but to get away from it as quickly as possible. But as he turned, something moved in his eye-corner. All his senses startled alert. He stopped.

Over to his right a thin, black horse was running across the ploughland towards the hill, its head down, neck stretched out. It seemed to be running on its toes like a cat, like a dog up to no good.

From the high point on which he stood the hill dipped slightly and rose to another crested point fringed with the tops of trees, three hundred yards to his right. As he watched it, the horse ran up that crest, showed against the sky—for a moment like a nightmarish leopard—and disappeared over the other side.

For several seconds he stared at the skyline, stunned by the unpleasantly strange impression the horse had made on him. Then the plastering beat of icy rain on his bare skull brought him to himself. The distance had vanished in a wall of grey. All around him the fields were jumping and streaming.

Holding his collar close and tucking his chin down into it he ran back over the hilltop towards the town-side, the lee-side, his feet sucking and splashing, at every stride plunging to the ankle.

This hill was shaped like a wave, a gently rounded back lifting out of the valley to a sharply crested, almost concave front hanging over the river meadows towards the town. Down this front, from the crest, hung two small woods separated by a fallow field. The near wood was nothing more than a quarry, circular, full of stones and bracken, with a few thorns and nondescript saplings, foxholes and rabbit holes. The other was rectangular, mainly a planting of scrub oak trees. Beyond the river smouldered the town like a great heap of blue cinders.

He ran along the top of the first wood and finding no shelter but the thin, leafless thorns of the hedge, dipped below the crest out of the wind and jogged along through thick grass to the wood of oaks. In blinding rain he lunged through the barricade of brambles at the wood's edge. The little crippled trees were small choice in the way of shelter, but at a sudden fierce thickening of the rain he took one at random and crouched down under the leaning trunk.

Still panting from his run, drawing his knees up tightly, he watched the bleak lines of rain, grey as hail, slanting through the boughs into the clumps of bracken and bramble. He felt hidden and safe. The sound of the rain as it rushed and lulled in the wood seemed to seal him in. Soon the chilly sheet lead of his suit became a tight, warm mould, and gradually he sank into a state of comfort that was all but trance, though the rain beat steadily on his exposed shoulders and trickled down the oak trunk on to his neck.

All around him the boughs angled down, glistening, black as iron. From their tips and elbows the drops hurried steadily, and the channels of the bark pulsed and gleamed. For a time he amused himself calculating the variation in rainfall by the variations in a dribble of water from a trembling twig-end two feet in front of his nose. He studied the twig, bringing dwarfs and continents and animals out of its scurfy bark. Beyond the boughs the blue shoal of the town was rising and falling, and darkening and fading again, in the pale, swaying backdrop of rain.

He wanted this rain to go on forever. Whenever it seemed to be drawing off he listened anxiously until it closed in again. As long as it lasted he was suspended from life and time. He didn't want to return to his sodden shoes and his possibly ruined suit and the walk back over that land of mud.

All at once he shivered. He hugged his knees to keep out the cold and found himself thinking of the horse. The hair on the nape of his neck prickled slightly. He remembered how it had run up to the crest and showed against the sky.

He tried to dismiss the thought. Horses wander about the countryside often enough. But the image of the horse as it had appeared against the sky stuck in his mind. It must have come over the crest just above the wood in which he was now sitting. To clear his mind, he twisted around and looked up the wood between the tree stems, to his left.

At the wood top, with the silvered grey light coming in behind it, the black horse was standing under the oaks, its head high and alert, its ears pricked, watching him.

TED HUGHES *The Rain-Horse*

Comprehension and Appreciation

1 Study the style of the passage. From the following list of adjectives choose *two* which, in your opinion, most fittingly characterise the language used: humorous, conversational, poetic, elegant, vigorous, rhetorical, forceful, pretentious, pompous.

2 Find examples of the writer's use of simile and metaphor and assess the effectiveness of each example.

3 What sentence do you consider most effective in this extract? Give your reasons.

4 How does the writer convey that the horse has a sense of mystery or fear about it?

5 What effect does the rain have on the man as he sits in the wood?

6 What kinds of trees are mentioned? What are we told about them?

7 Write an appreciation of this passage, paying special attention to the writer's use of language and of detail, and his physical descriptions of the horse, the rain, and the landscape.

Composition

8 This passage provides you with two characters in a particular setting. Start with the situation at the end of the passage and write the remainder of the story.

79

Write descriptions of these two scenes under the titles 'The Carnival' and 'Aldgate in the Rain'. A revision of the method outlined on page 81 will be of assistance.

80

Reduce this passage to note form with suitable headings and subheadings. Give the finished notes a title.

A teaching machine seeks to emulate the ideal teaching situation which is that of one teacher to one pupil and it does so in this manner.

A specialist in a subject takes the area of information to be imparted to the pupil and breaks it down into very short, logical and progressive steps. Each of these small steps requires some sort of answer or response from the pupil to signify that he has understood the step being made. The steps may be so small and so easily understood that it is impossible for a pupil to give a wrong answer to any question. This breaking down of information into short items or steps is known as programming, and each step with its question to the pupil is known as a frame.

The making of a programme is a slow process which involves testing, checking and rewriting over and over again until it is certain that there is no mistake in communication with the pupil.

Programmes may vary in their approach from the staircase or step-by-step type to the kind which offers the pupil a choice of answer to each question and then gives additional information if he selects the wrong answer. The former is known as a linear programme and the latter a branched programme. Linear programmes have a single question to be answered for each frame but branched programmes have a multiple-choice answer.

Much of the research on programming was carried out at Harvard University and two American psychologists, B. F. Skinner (linear programmes) and N. A. Crowther (multiple-choice answer) may be regarded as the fathers of the teaching machine movement.

The finished programme, on rolls of paper or film, may then be fed into any number of teaching machines in any number of schools, thus bringing thousands of pupils into individual contact with the mind of the subject-matter specialist.

The machine into which the programme is fed may be a complex mechanical device or a simple wooden box. Basically each has a window in which one frame appears at a time and some means by which the pupil can answer the related question without cheating. This may be done by writing the answer on paper which appears at another window and which disappears behind a transparent screen when the next question and the correct answer appear. In the more complex machines a frame of a branched programme may be answered by pushing one of a number of buttons. The correct button brings forward the next frame but an incorrect button will automatically display an additional frame with supplementary information which will enable the pupil to make the correct answer.

Programmes may also be supplied in book form, but the difficulty here, even with scrambled answers, is to prevent cheating by the pupil.

81

Peer Gynt Suites Nos 1 and 2 EDVARD GRIEG

SIDE NO 1	SIDE NO 2
SUITE NO 1 OP 46	SUITE NO 2 OP 55
1 Morning	1 Ingrid's Lament
2 The Death of Äse	2 Arabian dance
3 Anitra's Dance	3 The return of Peer Gynt
4 In the Hall of the Mountain King	4 Solveig's song

Malcolm Edwards conducting **The Washington Symphony Orchestra**

This is the basic information about a new recording of *Peer Gynt*—Suites Nos 1 and 2 which is to be issued by the Delta Record Company.

As an employee of the firm you have been asked to produce a sleeve for the record. This involves writing the information for one side of the sleeve and suggesting a suitable photograph or illustration for the other.

1 Make notes about Edvard Grieg and the *Peer Gynt* suites from books in the library. Include the basic information given above.
2 Invent several persuasive comments about the quality of the recording, the orchestra and the conductor.
3 Make arrangements to listen to a recording of the suites and then make further notes.
4 Arrange all the information you have collected into the best possible order and then expand it into a piece of continuous writing for the sleeve.
5 Either (*a*) make notes for a photograph or design which will interpret the music and the story, or (*b*) draw the rough sketch of your final idea for submission to the firm's Art Department.

Additional Exercises

The record company is also promoting a new popular singer called Tom Becket. He has had two records in the Top Twenty and has now recorded a long playing record with the provisional title 'Becket Sings Beatles Hits'.

Use your imagination and knowledge of popular music to write the sleeve notes for this record. Supply your own title and invent any other information you require.

82

Write a summary of the following passage in not more than 200 words.

In general, man regards insects as enemies rather than allies, and most economic entomologists devote a greater part of their time fighting the seemingly limitless variety of insect pests. But there is another side to the picture. In some cases insects can be used to destroy or limit the spread of troublesome weeds.

Man has learnt to his enormous cost the danger of upsetting the natural balance within local communities by importing non-native plants or wild animals. The introduction of the rabbit into Australia is a notorious example of this: less well known is the almost equally serious importation into Australia of prickly-pear cacti. Both rabbits and cacti had no apparent enemies to keep them in check: as a result they multiplied prodigiously and developed into very serious pests. In both cases their eventual suppression was due mainly to the importation of insects— the mosquito that spread myxomatosis among the rabbits, and the moth that cleared the cacti.

The many species of the prickly-pear cacti are all natives of South and Central America. They are useful as hedging plants and their fruits are edible, and for these reasons they have been introduced into many parts of the world, often with unfortunate results. In Australia the plants found both the climate and the soil suitable, and they quickly began to spread. At the peak of the invasion, in 1919, about 60 million acres of fertile land had been rendered useless and the cacti were estimated to be spreading at a million acres a year.

In 1920 entomologists were sent to investigate insects connected with the prickly pear. Altogether 145 different insects were found, all of them dependent for food on prickly pear or other species of cactus.

Quite a number of them had to be rejected because it was found that they could also sustain themselves on tomatoes, peaches, apples, figs and bananas. About 18 'safe' species were finally selected for trials. Several of these managed to establish themselves in Australia, and one species, a moth from Argentina named *Cactoblastis cactorum*, very quickly outstripped all the others and became the most important enemy of the prickly pear.

This moth is brown-grey in colour and measures about an inch and a half across the wings. The female lays its eggs in long chains that it attaches to the spines of the prickly pear. When the red-and-black caterpillars hatch out they burrow into the cacti and feed on the sappy tissues, leaving only skin and fibres.

In 1926 more than two-and-a-quarter million eggs were fixed to cactus plants throughout the infested areas. The following year six-and-a-half million eggs were sent out. By 1929 hundreds of acres of the cactus had already collapsed, and the introduction of the *Cactoblastis* appeared to be an outstanding success.

By 1935 almost all the cacti had been destroyed, roots and all. Since then *Cactoblastis* has decreased to a mere fraction of its former numbers owing to the shortage of prickly pear. But it retains its capacity for rapid increase when conditions are favourable, and so continues as a natural control of the prickly pear. The lost acres have been reclaimed and are now in full use for grazing and farming.

L. HUGH NEWMAN *Man and Insects*

83

Imagine that you are employed by an advertising agency that is promoting a new advertising campaign for a manufacturer of breakfast cereals.

The agency's market research revealed that consumers of breakfast cereal always read the back of the packet whilst it is on the table, and this led the agency to the idea of service to the community by providing Instant Culture on the back of the packet.

The campaign is to be presented in the following three stages and under the slogan of 'Breakfast Time is Culture Time'.

1 *Instant Literature Series* Summaries of famous books to give everyone an acquaintance with the classics without having to read them.
2 *Instant Sculpture Series* Plastic moulds for the reproduction of well-known pieces of sculpture presented free with each packet. This will enable consumers to make their own Instant Rodin or Michelangelo.
3 *Instant Art Appreciation Series* Reproductions of three famous paintings, with explanation and brief notes on the painter, on the back of each packet.

The work allocated to you is as follows:

1 Write summaries of two famous books for inclusion in the Instant Literature Series. An example is given below.

The Grapes of Wrath by John Steinbeck

This famous novel tells of the hardships of the Joads, a farming family, who are driven out of their home in the Oklahoma Dust Bowl region by the big corporations who own the land and wish to mechanise its cultivation. They set out in a dilapidated Hudson truck on a trek to California in search of work as migrant fruit-pickers. The grandparents die on the way, and on arrival the family are hounded by police, sheriffs, labour contractors and strikers. They meet violence with violence and Tom, the Joad son, kills a striker. The story finishes with the family facing starvation and defeat, but still retaining their courage.

2 Find pictures of works by two famous sculptors and write a brief description of each to accompany the plastic mould.
3 Stage Three starts with a packet devoted to The Essential Picasso. Choose three paintings by Picasso for reproduction and write a short description of each painting. In addition write a short summarised biography of Picasso.

84

In this exercise you are required to write from two different points of view.

Place yourself in the position of the Jamaican girl in the photograph and try to understand her feelings and attitudes. What was your reason for coming to Britain and what were your first reactions to the country? Did you have problems of language and understanding, did the weather affect your health and did you have housing difficulties? How do you get along with the people here? Have you been refused service in a shop or café? Is your life in Britain more enjoyable than in your home country? Is your stay permanent or are you going back?

Write an account telling what it is like to be a coloured immigrant in Britain.

Now place yourself in the position of the passing workman. Your reactions to coloured people in Britain may be assessed from the facial expression. Do you feel that their background and way of life is too different from yours and that they don't even speak understandable English? Is it your opinion that coloured people take jobs that your own people should have? Do you feel that they live in crowded conditions and are content with a lower standard of living than yours?

In the words of your imagined character express his feelings, attitudes and views on coloured people in Britain.

THREE STANDING
HENRY MOORE

PRESENTED TO THE LCC BY THE CONTEMP

85

This piece of sculpture is called 'Three Standing Figures' and it was carved from Darley Dale stone by Henry Moore. Study the photograph and the extract from *The Meaning of Art* and then answer the questions.

What distinguishes sculpture as an art? Obviously, its material and technique: sculpture is the art of carving or cutting a material of relative hardness. So much is implied in the word itself, and no extension of this definition is necessary. When we come to the actual working-out of this process we are faced with the fundamental question: What is the sculptor to carve? For the last 400 years artists have said: We will carve a block of stone or marble into the very image of Alderman Jones, or of Miss Simpkins posing as Venus, of a dying lion or a flying duck; and man has marvelled at the ingenuity with which the artist has accomplished this difficult aim. The aim of a sculptor like Henry Moore has nothing at all in common with this. He has no regard at all for the appearance of the object (if there is one) which inspires his work of art. His first concern is for his material. If that material is stone, he will consider the structure of the stone, its degree of hardness, the way it reacts to his chisel. He will consider how this stone has reacted to natural forces like wind and water, for these in the course of time have revealed the inherent qualities of the stone. Finally, he will ask himself what form he can best realise in the particular block of stone he has before him; and if this form is, say, the reclining figure of a woman, he will imagine (and this is the act which calls for his peculiar sensibility or insight) what a reclining woman would look like if flesh and blood were translated into the stone before him—the stone which has its own principles of form and structure. The woman's body might then, as it actually does in some of Moore's figures, take on the appearance of a range of hills. Sculpture, therefore, is not a *reduplication* of form and feature; it is rather the *translation of meaning* from one material into another. That, it seems to me, is a simple enough statement, not difficult to accept; yet it is the only key that is needed for the understanding of sculpture like this of Henry Moore's, and it is therefore incomprehensible why so much difficulty should be experienced by the ordinary man in the presence of such work.

HERBERT READ *The Meaning of Art*

1 In which newspaper would a photograph like this be reproduced? What is the underlying assumption about the reader's attitude to modern sculpture?

2 State clearly and briefly the difference between the aim of Henry Moore and the aim of earlier sculptors.

3 Why do some of Moore's female figures 'take on the appearance of a range of hills'?

4 What, according to Herbert Read, is the key needed for the understanding of Henry Moore's sculpture?

5 Explain the meaning of the following words and phrases as used in the passage:

reduplication of form and feature
incomprehensible
inherent qualities
peculiar sensibility
fundamental

6 Study the standing figure that faces you and note that Moore has simplified the detail of the head, hands, feet and clothing in the interests of final effect. Does this satisfy you or would you prefer to see more detail or less detail? Give your reasons.

7 Write a clear, factual description of the figures you are able to see.

8 Arrange under two headings the advantages and the disadvantages of displaying sculpture in the open.

9 With the help of the passage write a simple explanation of this work for the benefit of the puzzled 'ordinary' man in the photograph.

10 Give reasons why you do or do not think that Henry Moore is successful in the 'translation of meaning from one material into another'.

86

Read the following extract and then answer the questions that follow it.

LINCOLN: Oh! Good afternoon, ladies.

MRS OTHERLY: Good afternoon, Mr President.

LINCOLN: Good afternoon, good afternoon.

MRS BLOW: And is there any startling news, Mr President?

LINCOLN: Madam, every morning when I wake up, and say to myself, a hundred, or two hundred, or a thousand of my countrymen will be killed today, I find it startling.

MRS BLOW: Oh yes, to be sure. But I mean, is there any good news.

LINCOLN: Yes. There is news of victory. They lost twenty-seven hundred men —we lost eight hundred.

MRS BLOW: How splendid.

LINCOLN: Thirty-five hundred.

MRS BLOW: Oh, but you mustn't talk like that, Mr President. There were only eight hundred that mattered.

LINCOLN: The world is larger than your heart, madam.

MRS BLOW: Now the dear President is becoming whimsical, Mrs Lincoln.

MRS OTHERLY: Mr President.

LINCOLN: Yes, ma'am.

MRS OTHERLY: I don't like to impose upon your hospitality. I know how difficult everything is for you. But one has to take one's opportunities. May I ask you a question?

LINCOLN: Certainly, ma'am.

MRS OTHERLY: Isn't it possible for you to stop this war? In the name of a suffering country, I ask you that.

MRS BLOW: I'm sure such a question would never have entered my head.

LINCOLN: It is a perfectly right question. Ma'am, I have but one thought always —how can this thing be stopped? But we must ensure the integrity of the Union. In two years war has become an hourly bitterness to me. I believe I suffer no less than any man. But it must be endured. The cause was a right one two years ago. It is unchanged.

MRS OTHERLY: I know you are noble and generous. But I believe, that war must be wrong under any circumstances, for any cause.

MRS BLOW: I'm afraid the President would have but little encouragement if he listened often to this kind of talk.

LINCOLN: I beg you not to harass yourself, madam. Ma'am, I too believe war to be wrong. It is the weakness and the jealousy and the folly of men that make a thing so wrong possible. But we are all weak, and jealous, and foolish. That's how the world is, ma'am, and we cannot outstrip the world. Some of the worst of us are sullen, aggressive still—just clumsy, greedy pirates. Some of us have grown out of that. But the best of us have an instinct to resist aggression if it won't listen to persuasion. You may say it's a wrong instinct. I don't know. But it's there, and it's there in millions of good men. I don't believe it's a wrong instinct. I believe that the world must come to wisdom slowly. It is for us who hate aggression to persuade men always and earnestly against it, and hope that, little by little, they will hear us. But in the meantime there will come moments when the aggressors will force the instinct to resistance to act. Then we must act earnestly, praying always in our courage that never again will this thing happen. And then we must turn again, and again, and again to persuasion. This appeal to force is the misdeed of an imperfect world. But we are imperfect. We must strive to purify the world, but we must not think ourselves pure above the world. When I had this thing to decide, it would have been easy to say, 'No, I will have none of it; it is evil, and I will not touch it.' But that would have decided nothing, and I saw what I believed to be the truth as I now put it to you, ma'am. It's a forlorn thing for any man to have this responsibility in his heart. I may see wrongly, but that's how I see.

MRS OTHERLY: Thank you, Mr President, for what you've said. I must try to think about it. But I always believed war to be wrong. I didn't want my boy to go because I believed war to be wrong. But he would. This paper came to me last week. From his Colonel. You may read it, Mr Lincoln.

LINCOLN: 'Dear Madam, I regret to inform you that . . .' Ma'am, there are times when no man may speak. I grieve for you, I grieve for you.

MRS OTHERLY: I think I will go. You don't mind my saying what I did?

LINCOLN: We are all poor creatures, ma'am. Think kindly of me. Mary, will you . . . ?

MRS LINCOLN: Of course, Abraham. Mrs Otherly . . .

MRS BLOW: Of course it's very sad for her, poor woman. But she makes her trouble worse by these perverted views, doesn't she? And, I hope you will show no signs of weakening, Mr President, till it has been made impossible for those shameful rebels to hold up their heads again. Goliath says you ought to make a proclamation that no mercy will be shown to them afterwards. I'm sure I shall never speak to one of them again. Well I must be going. I'll see Mrs Lincoln as I go out. Good afternoon, Mr President.

LINCOLN: Good afternoon, madam. And I'd like to offer ye a word of advice. That poor mother told me what she thought. I don't agree with her, but I honour her. She's wrong, but she is noble. You've told me what you think. I don't agree with you, and I'm ashamed of you and your like. You, who have sacrificed nothing, babble about destroying the South while other people conquer it. I accepted this war with a sick heart, and I've a heart that's near to breaking every day. I accepted it in the name of humanity, and just and merciful dealing, and the hope of love and charity on earth. And you come to me, talking of revenge and destruction, and malice, and enduring hate. These gentle people are mistaken, but they are mistaken cleanly, and in a great name. It is you that dishonour the cause for which we stand—it is you who would make it a mean and little thing. Good afternoon.

JOHN DRINKWATER *Abraham Lincoln*

Comprehension, Interpretation and Comment

1 Suggest a short appropriate title for the extract.
2 Explain the force of Lincoln's 'Thirty-five hundred'.
3 What does Lincoln mean when he says 'The world is larger than your heart, madam'?
4 Convey in your own words the attitude of Mrs Blow towards the Southern rebels.
5 Give brief character sketches of (*a*) Mrs Blow, (*b*) Mrs Otherly, and (*c*) Lincoln, as they are revealed in this extract.
6 Summarise the main idea of the extract in one sentence.
7 Give in your own words the attitude of Lincoln towards war.
8 In what circumstances, if any, do you feel that war is justifiable?
9 How convincing do you find the arguments in favour of a policy of non-violence as a means of managing conflict?
10 Give three reasons why you do or do not think that the 'roots of war' are to be found in the nature of man himself.

Composition

Either

Discuss the following both as an ideal and its actual exercise:

Never resist the evildoer by force, do not meet violence with violence. If they beat you, endure it; if they take your possessions, yield them up; if they compel you to work, work; and if they wish to take from you what you consider to be yours, give it up.

L. N. TOLSTOY *What I Believe*

Or

Discuss one of the following:

(*a*) The role of an armed International Police Force.

(*b*) The case for an unarmed World Peace Brigade.

87

The following table shows the attitudes of women to certain groups of the mass media. Write in the form of a continuous statement the conclusions you draw from the figures.

Selected Functions of Media Groups *proportions of all women*

'Which of these do you think are good. . . .'	PAPERS %	RADIO %	WWM* %	TV %	WMM† %	NONE %
When you want to enjoy yourself?	13	30	19	57	11	5
For finding out what other people are doing?	53	14	11	39	5	2
When you feel in a serious mood?	23	24	11	18	7	21
When you want to have a good laugh?	3	23	5	72	1	9
For finding out what is worth buying?	25	5	33	24	18	14
For advertisements which interest you?	27	1	29	31	18	14
When you want to get away from it all?	4	15	14	19	8	42
For giving you a fresh outlook and ideas?	12	8	38	24	27	12
For keeping up with world events?	63	17	1	49	1	1
For useful information and advice?	23	17	37	21	19	10
For what interests you as a woman?	13	12	55	19	32	6
For what interests you as a housewife?	14	15	48	24	29	7
Average number of functions	2·73	1·81	3·01	3·97	1·79	1·43

* Women's weekly magazines. † Women's monthly magazines.

Source: ODHAMS: a new measurement study of women's weekly magazines.

Alistair MacLean...
Your passport to nerve-shattering suspense and action-packed excitement

Accept
H.M.S. ULYSSES
FREE
as your introductory gift.

HERON BOOKS

.... too thrilling to relax with ... breathless action ... gripping suspense. Compulsive reading .... This is Alistair Maclean.

MacLean's talent is so accurately mirrored in our FREE introductory volume. A story of the war-time Russian convoys ... the life-line of Britain's allies at the time of their greatest peril. And this is your opportunity to live alongside the officers and ratings aboard H.M.S. Ulysses. You'll realise that from the captain down to the most junior cabin-boy these are not unusual people.

Not the dashing dragoon or knight errant ... the crew of Ulysses are ordinary, unremarkable, worried men. They're cold, desperate, hungry ... sick with fear ... and this is what makes them heroes; what makes them recognisable and so understandable. You will have gathered by now that we are talking about a very special author. Alistair MacLean, a Scots school-master, who with the publication of his first novel was catapulted into the literary limelight by an avalanche of praise from the world's press critics.

MacLean believes in involvement. He grabs his readers by the scruff of the neck and wrenches them headlong into the storm-centre of the action ... where the pace is hottest ... the risks gravest ... and dare-devilment is as natural as breathing. His is a very special talent ... the ability to make the printed page swim before your eyes, such is your desperation to keep up with the excitement. Stock up on the mid-night oil before you start a MacLean, his are not the sort of novels you can browse through, they are quite definitely 'one sitting' stories ... books you simply can't put down.

Heron Books, Heron House, London SW18 2LX.

Superb Books Bound To Be Enjoyed

We know that action-packed novels such as these will be read time and time again, not only by you and your family, but also by your book borrowing friends. All this means far more handling than the average book receives, so we have made sure that this doesn't mean extra wear and tear ... after all these are far from average books. Each volume is sumptuously bound in navy-blue Kidron, almost as soft to the touch as doe skin glove and yet tough enough to withstand the complex hand acids that can stain ordinary leather. And the bookbinder's art didn't stop there. This is an edition to honour Britain's best selling author. Special artists were commissioned to capture the pace and excitement of MacLean's spell-binding stories. The end-papers are heavy and luxurious. There are silken head and tail bands and a bound-in silken bookmark. Embellished with lavish golden tooling on the covers and spine, The Alistair MacLean Collection will surely bring a thrilling touch of excitement to your library.

Start collecting this exciting series with a FREE GIFT

As your thrilling introduction to Alistair MacLean we will send you H.M.S. Ulysses together with Where Eagles Dare ... yours to read and enjoy for 10 days before making a decision of any kind. If you are not absolutely delighted with this author's tremendously exciting work you may return both volumes within 10 days post paid and owe nothing.

Otherwise you may keep H.M.S. Ulysses as a FREE GIFT and for Where Eagles Dare you will be asked to pay only the special subscriber's price of £1.55 (plus p&p). Then approximately one month later, unless you notify us to the contrary, we shall send you, without obligation to accept, the other fourteen matching volumes in the collection ... all on approval and with the right to pay for those you accept at *the rate of one volume a month*.

FREE GIFT COUPON
Offer closes 19th March 1974

To: The Alistair MacLean Collection
Heron Books, A Division of Leisure Arts Ltd.
Dept. 722/024 *Heron House, London SW18 2LX.*

Please send me, with no purchase obligation, H.M.S. Ulysses together with Where Eagles Dare to read and enjoy for 10 days. If I am not absolutely thrilled I may return both volumes within 10 days and owe nothing. Otherwise H.M.S. Ulysses is mine FREE, and for Where Eagles Dare I will pay the Special Subscriber's Price of only £1.55 (plus p&p).
Then approximately one month later I will receive, on 10 days approval, the remaining 14 volumes in the collection. Those I decide to keep, will be mine for the same Special Subscriber's Price of £1.55 (plus p&p). Although I will have the benefit of receiving all the remaining volumes at the same time I CAN PAY FOR THEM AT A VOLUME AT A TIME AT MONTHLY INTERVALS.

NAME _____

SEND NO MONEY NOW

ADDRESS _____

D5

——— Div. of Leisure Arts Ltd. - Reg'd No. 689088 ———

Other Thrilling Stories In The Alistair MacLean Collection ...

The Guns of Navarone	Puppet On A Chain
Fear Is The Key	The Satan Bug
Force 10 From Navarone	South By Java Head
Ice Station Zebra	When Eight Bells Toll
The Golden Rendezvous	Caravan To Vaccares
The Last Frontier	The Dark Crusaders
Night Without End	Bear Island

88

Make a careful study of the advertisement reproduced on page 176 and then answer the following questions.

1 Describe briefly the type of person likely to be attracted by the headline.
2 What overall picture does the advertisement try to convey?
3 Comment on the effectiveness of the design and typography of the advertisement.
4 Give two or three examples of how the words of the copy recreate the experience of enjoying the books.
5 Consider the actual information given in the copy. How much of the copy is informational and how much persuasive?
6 It has been said by some advertisers that 'the more you tell the more you sell'. What are your reactions to lengthy copy in advertisements?
7 Think carefully about the copy and then write a paragraph or two giving your own views.
8 Ask your teacher to lead a class discussion on the language of the advertisement. Note the points that emerge from the discussion and in addition formulate one or two opinions of your own. Supply a title and write an analysis of the language used.
9 Write persuasive copy for a similar but shorter advertisement that deals with a collection of books about Victorian England.
10 Collect advertisements that give information about book clubs. What does membership of the clubs entail? Are there advantages in membership? Compare a book club edition with a paperback edition. Which is better value? Are you in favour of books being chosen for you or do you prefer to choose your own? What is your opinion of some of the books selected by the clubs? Do you consider that book clubs offer a valuable service by bringing books into households which, for some reason or other, would not otherwise bother to build up a private library of their own? Where did book clubs originate? Which was the first book club in Britain? How many major book clubs are there in Britain today? Obtain as much information as you can and then present your study as a piece of extended writing.

	GOLF	FISHING	TENNIS	SWIMMING	SAILING	MOTOR RACING	CLIMBING	PONY TREKKING	RAMBLING	DANCING	CINEMA	CARAVAN SITE	SANDY BEACH	PEBBLE BEACH	LAKE/RIVER SETTING	MOUNTAIN/HILL	FOREST/WOOD	ANCIENT MONUMENTS	YOUTH HOSTEL
Antrim	•	•	•		•					•	•				•	•		•	
Ballymena		•	•					•		•	•								
Belfast		•	•	•	•	•				•	•				•			•	•
Cushendall		•	•	•	•		•						•		•				•
Downpatrick		•	•	•				•		•	•						•	•	•
Giant's Causeway		•	•		•				•				•						•
Glenarm		•	•							•				•		•			•
Kilkeel		•	•		•					•			•						•
Larne		•	•	•	•					•	•				•				•
Lurgan		•	•		•				•	•	•								
Newry		•				•				•	•				•	•		•	•
Rostrevor		•		•		•			•						•				•

178

89

The trio in the photograph are on a motoring holiday in Northern Ireland and are planning the next stage of their journey.

Imagine that you and two friends have been sent by a travel magazine on a similar holiday in return for an article to be published by them on your return. The following conditions were laid down:

Time Fourteen days in Northern Ireland.

Route Cross by the short sea route to Larne in County Antrim and then cover 1,000 miles visiting the following places—Glenarm, Cushendall, Giant's Causeway, Ballymena, Antrim, Larne, Lurgan, Newry, Rostrevor, Kilkeel, Downpatrick and Belfast. All travelling in Northern Ireland must be done by car.

Accommodation The fourteen overnight stops to be made at local hotels, inns and boarding houses.

The preceding table will give information about some of the amenities at the places to be visited and additional information can be obtained from the library or nearest travel agency. The RAC and AA Handbooks will be found useful, as will the *Oxford Travel Atlas of Britain* and any good Road Atlas of Great Britain.

Write the article for the magazine. Provide a title, a description of the places visited and a map of the journey.

90

Study this picture of a crowd at Battersea Park and then answer the questions which follow.

1. Supply a suitable title.
2. Write two sentences which describe the general impression conveyed by the crowd.
3. Why did the photographer take this particular picture?
4. In which season of the year and at what time of day could this photograph have been taken?
5. Explain the use of the barriers in the foreground for the benefit of a person who has never seen them.
6. Write a brief report explaining the composition of this crowd. Mention age groups, social class, sex, etc.
7. There are some forty people in this group. Study them carefully and then make comments on each of the following:
   (*a*) the wearing of spectacles;
   (*b*) hats;
   (*c*) smoking;
   (*d*) cameras;
   (*e*) jewellery.
8. Write a brief report on either the men's clothing or the women's hair styles.
9. Write a short description of the young man standing behind the 'No Waiting' sign.
10. Choose any couple from this photograph to represent a man and a woman who were seen shoplifting but escaped without being caught. Write a careful description of them for the benefit of a policeman searching the crowd.

91

Read carefully the following passage, and then answer the questions set on it.

He looked northward towards Howth. The sea had fallen below the line of seawrack on the shallow side of the breakwater and already the tide was running out fast along the foreshore. Already one long oval bank of sand lay warm and dry amid the wavelets. Here and there warm isles of sand gleamed above the shallow tides and about the isles and around the long bank and amid the shallow currents of the bridge were lightclad figures, wading and delving.

In a few moments he was barefoot, his stockings folded in his pockets, and his canvas shoes dangling by their knotted laces over his shoulders and, picking a pointed salteaten stick out of the jetsam among the rocks, he clambered down the slope of the breakwater.

There was a long rivulet in the strand and, as he waded slowly up its course, he wondered at the endless drift of seaweed. Emerald and black and russet and olive, it moved beneath the current, swaying and turning. The water of the rivulet was dark with endless drift and mirrored the high-drifting clouds. The clouds were drifting above him silently and silently the sea-tangle was drifting below him; and the grey warm air was still: and a new wild life was singing in his veins.

JAMES JOYCE *Portrait of the Artist as a Young Man*

1 Study the style of the passage. From the following list of adjectives choose *two* which best describe the language used: conversational, vivid, detailed, impressionistic, pompous, elegant, precise, poetic.
2 Show how the second paragraph is linked with the first.
3 Comment on the writer's use of adjectival and adverbial phrases.
4 Which clause in the passage indicates that the man referred to is at some point of crisis or excitement in his life?
5 Is this a description of (i) a seashore scene, (ii) a mental experience, or (iii) a combination of both? Give your reasons.
6 Quote words and phrases from the passage which prepare the reader for the last ten words.
7 Is the writing in this passage objective (the writer's personality kept in the background), or subjective (the writer's personal impressions clearly shown)?
8 Supply a suitable title for the passage.

92

Choose a TV crime drama from next week's *Radio* or *TV Times*. Watch the programme carefully and study the character of the villain by making notes based on the outline given below. Use your notes to write a character sketch of the villain.

1 Villain's main characteristics
- (*a*) apparent age
- (*b*) nationality
- (*c*) social status
- (*d*) habitual or casual criminal
- (*e*) member of gang or freelance
- (*f*) relationship to hero

2 Villain's social background and habits
- (*a*) underworld
- (*b*) high society
- (*c*) business
- (*d*) politics
- (*e*) domestic
- (*f*) drinking
- (*g*) gambling
- (*h*) women
- (*i*) drugs

3 Villain's crime and motive
- (*a*) theft
- (*b*) forgery
- (*c*) non-fatal violence
- (*d*) murder
- (*e*) power
- (*f*) vengeance
- (*g*) money
- (*h*) sex

4 Villain's punishment
- (*a*) death
- (*b*) prison
- (*c*) non-fatal violence

93

Read the following passage and then make a set of notes that would act as an aid to memory for answering an examination question on the subject.

The principal venereal diseases are gonorrhoea and syphilis. The following introductory statement is taken from a booklet entitled *Sexual Promiscuity*, published by the SPCK:

'Venereal disease is nearly always contracted in sexual intercourse with an infected person. It is a fair assumption that anyone who is prepared to have intercourse with a stranger or with a casual acquaintance has had similar contacts in the past with individuals who may be harbouring such infection. The danger of contracting venereal disease from promiscuous intercourse is very great.'

The germ that causes syphilis finds its way through the skin, or the mucous membrane, on any part of the body and very soon gets into the blood stream, by which it is carried to every part of the body.

The first sign that a person has become infected is the appearance of a sore, or ulcer, usually on the genital area, but sometimes on lips, fingers, or breasts. The sore will appear wherever the germs gain entry to the body. Usually the sore appears about three weeks after infection, but the interval might be as long as three months. Like anything else in syphilis, the sore might be hidden away in the vagina or on the neck of the womb in the female, or it may be so small and painless as to escape notice completely in either male or female.

Usually some six to twelve weeks pass before other signs of syphilis show. It is during this time that a blood test for syphilis becomes positive. A rash might develop on the body, face or hands and, because it does not itch, it could pass unnoticed. Ulcers might appear in the mouth and throat and the voice might become hoarse. The glands in the neck and armpits and groins might become enlarged, and the hair might fall out in patches. In spite of all this the infected persons might still feel quite fit and, because all the things described are painless, might not seek treatment. In this stage, which is known as secondary syphilis, the patients are most contagious and will infect anyone coming into close contact with them, since every syphilitic ulcer contains the germs; if the ulcers are on the lips or in the mouth the disease might be spread by kissing people. In this way anyone might become innocently infected. The disease can also be transmitted by the fingers in heavy petting.

If infected persons do not seek treatment this stage might last for several weeks or months and then gradually all the signs and symptoms disappear; the skin heals, the hair grows again and the sore disappears. The infected persons feel perfectly well, but the germs of syphilis are still in their bodies, burying themselves in the bones, brain, blood vessels and, in fact, in every part of the body; they will stay there for months or years before the infected patient feels anything else wrong.

This stage of syphilis is known as the latent or sleeping stage. The only way of finding it then is by a blood test. The infected person might seem perfectly well, he might lead a normal life (including normal work) yet all the time the germs of syphilis are burying themselves in every part of his (or her) body. Later they will cause a great deal of damage. How much damage the disease causes depends upon the patients' resistance, and on this also depends the length of time before any symptoms of what we call 'late syphilis' are seen.

Any time from five to forty and more years after infection large painless ulcers might develop anywhere on the body. These are known as gummata. They look as if they should be painful but seldom are. The skin and bone can be destroyed and extensive scarring follows as a result.

It could be as long as fifteen or twenty years after infection that the patient begins to suffer from disease of the heart, and ultimately the wall of the big blood vessel leading from the heart could be so weakened that it bursts and the patient dies. Similarly, it could be that twenty or even thirty years after infection the patients begin to lose control of their senses; they lose their memory and they might be found by friends, relatives or the people with whom they work to be mentally unstable, and finish up by being admitted to a mental ward. This means that the disease has damaged part of the brain and, if there has been a long delay between the appearance of the first signs of mental disturbance and admission to hospital, this damage might be permanent. However, if it is taken in time there is no reason why they should not, after treatment, return to a normal life. If other parts of the nervous system are affected the patient may develop what is known as locomotor ataxia or tabes dorsalis, which shows itself in many ways and might lead to deafness, blindness or paralysis.

There is no need to go into great detail in describing these diseases since their many signs and symptoms would be recognised only by the doctor. All that needs to be known is that so long as the patient seeks treatment early enough, even these complications in syphilis can be arrested, and many of them could be cured completely.

Venereal Disease—A Simple Explanation by PHILIP S. SILVER

94

Write an article discussing the benefits derived from the exploration of space. Use the information given below, though you need not include all of it in your article. You may also use other information if you wish, but you must make use of some of the following:

(a) The exploration of space has affected everyone's life; it will continue to affect our lives more and more.

(b) All of us come into daily contact with some product or by-product which is the result of space research.

(c) People all over the world are affected by (i) weather forecast by satellite, (ii) navigation by satellite, and (iii) communication by satellite.

(d) Satellites are determining exact distances and precise shapes of land and sea areas on Earth, and are also making astronomical observations.

(e) The whole of mankind will benefit from the research work in aerospace medicine, e.g. human behaviour under great stress, emotion and fatigue, and the treatment of heart and blood illnesses.

(f) Research on space feeding and nutrition will influence future food and agricultural processes, e.g. synthetic and new foods, new methods of food growing, and the compression of large quantities of calories into small food capsules.

(g) The Apollo voyages to the Moon demonstrated man's capability for interplanetary travel. Such travel will be necessary in the distant future when life on earth becomes impossible and man has to find a way out of his solar system in order to survive.

(h) Space travel has changed man's perspectives. From the depths of space the earth has been seen for what it is: a tiny raft floating in a vast eternal silence. This new notion of the earth will change men's conception of themselves and of each other.

95

Turn back to page 165 and refresh your memory on the 'Breakfast Time is Culture Time' campaign. Finish your allocation of the work by completing the following:

1 Invent a brand name for a new breakfast cereal. Bear in mind the work on word association and the creation of good images on page 45.

2 Write advertising slogans, using your brand name or the word 'Culture', and base each one on the following methods:

(a) Exploitation of fear, ie, fear of illness, fear of losing one's job, or fear of what the neighbours think, eg, 'Do you suffer from Culture starvation?', or 'We can't possibly invite the Athertons, we haven't got Culture'.

(b) Appeal as a status symbol, eg, 'The Cereal that goes with Success', or 'Top People are Cultured People'.

(c) To parents through children, eg, 'Mother! Can you be sure that your children are getting enough Culture?', or 'Pass the Culture, Mum'.

(d) To people in the 'middle income' bracket, eg, 'Get ahead faster with Culture', or 'The cereal that's setting the trend'.

3 *Either*, draw a strip cartoon, complete with captions, of a young wife whose marriage was nearly wrecked because she failed to remain as cultured as her husband, *or*, write a short script on the same theme for a television commercial.

4 Write copy for a magazine display advertisement. An example, using two methods of appeal, is given below.

Don't worry if you can't afford a second car or a built-in stereo-unit. Just so long as you have a shelf and one wall to call your own, you can outsymbol the status brigade with Culture. Your collection of Instant Art and Instant Sculpture is this year's most successful way to upset the Joneses. Give your room that top-income-bracket air with Culture. Culture is provided by Puffed Sago, the breakfast cereal that makes Breakfast Time Culture Time.

5 An Instant Music stage of the campaign was considered by the agency and finally turned down because of the technical difficulties. Take the following two examples as a starting-point and make a serious report on the possibility of using Instant Music with a variety of products in future advertising campaigns.

(a) A musical cigarette packet that plays a theme from a symphony twenty times a day.

(b) Packaging along the lines of a musical-box which would play a tune on being opened.

96

Papermaking

A careful reader of this passage will note that it can be shortened and improved. For example, the two phases of papermaking are mentioned and then the second phase is described first. In addition there is repetition, ambiguity and a curious style of writing.

Work out the best order for the facts and reduce the passage to less than 200 of your own words. Aim for clear, concise sentences and paragraphs.

Fundamentally, paper is a species of cloth—originally all paper was made from waste cloth of one kind or another. The original paper made by the Chinese, who discovered papermaking as we know it today, was probably made from old fish nets.

The process consists of two distinct phases:

1 The production of the fibre.
2 The actual making of the paper.

The making of the paper consists of taking fibres of a vegetable origin and pounding them in the presence of water in something which is in the nature of an ordinary pestle and mortar, and under those conditions the fibres gradually break down and combine with the water, involving chemical processes which even today are imperfectly understood. Animal fibres such as sheep's wool won't work.

The pounded fibres are further diluted with water until there is perhaps only one part of fibre to one hundred of water and the whole is measured out carefully into accurate quantities and then is run through, evenly distributed, a cloth. The fibre, etc. stays on top of the cloth and the water runs through. The fibre, you will appreciate, will be lying in every different direction possible and when this is very nearly drained, the operator gives the frame holding the cloth a characteristic shake which more or less makes all the fibres interlock, so increasing the strength of the paper. The original method in China and the East was that the cloths were set out in the sun to dry and when they were dried the paper was peeled off the surface of the cloth.

Under modern conditions the basic principle is still the same—we still pound the fibres in the presence of water, the only difference is that it is done in a rotary arrangement, something like a paddle of a ship in a trough, and the fibres going round and round.

After this process has been continued for several hours, the fibres are diluted with water and then run on to an endless wire cloth, the water in the very dilute material passes through the wire cloth leaving the fibre on top of the wire cloth. The fibre is then continuously mangled, lifted off on an endless web, dried over steam-heated cylinders and rolled up.

This is fundamentally the same principle as was used in China perhaps 20,000 years ago, except that the process is now highly mechanised.

Under today's conditions the demand for paper is so great that there is not nearly enough textile wastes available, and the types of vegetable fibres which are available are too expensive for making cheap paper.

About one hundred years ago it was discovered that it was quite easy to extract the fibre from many forms of vegetable growth where the fibres were very short and ideally adapted for papermaking insofar as they were already partially broken down by the very nature of the plant they grew in.

Most paper is made from trees and certain types of naturally growing grasses like esparto grass and bamboo, and the process consists of boiling under pressure those woods and grasses with chemicals which have the property of dissolving the flesh portion of the plant and at the same time not attacking the fibrous portion of the plant.

It will be apparent that the selection of the particular chemical to use is all-important as it must be sufficiently strong to destroy all the flesh portion of the plant and at the same time not destroy the fibre portion.

Over the years a number of chemicals have been discovered which are very well adapted for this purpose, and today most paper such as used in school books, writing paper, wallpaper and newspaper and so on is made from trees and to a limited extent from grasses like esparto grass and bamboo.

This product after it is reduced to fibre is known as pulp and is today a very, very big article in international commerce. Countries where trees grow freely, such as Canada, Norway, Sweden and Finland have developed a very big business in the manufacture of pulp and this shows signs of being an important export from some tropical countries as gum (eucalyptus) is specially good for making pulp.

Much waste paper is salvaged for re-manufacture, but normally salvaged paper is used for making cheaper grades of paper. Cardboard boxes, for example, are made from salvaged paper.

Papermaking is a mass-production industry and there are few commodities in this world so cheap as paper when it is expressed in the cost per square yard. It is perhaps one hundred times cheaper than the cheapest cloth available, which would make any pretence of doing the same job. Whilst it is not nearly so durable as cloth and particularly has very little strength if wet, it is one of the most important commodities in everyday life, in the home, school and factory, and without paper it would be almost impossible to conduct life as we know it today.

97

For this assignment you will need a copy of your local newspaper. Make a careful study of the paper and then answer the following questions.

1 How many column inches are devoted to (i) advertisements, (ii) photographs, (iii) news?
2 How much space is allocated to advertisements dealing with (i) shops, (ii) cinemas, (iii) coach firms, (iv) classified?
3 How much of the news is concerned with (i) sport, (ii) local government, (iii) court cases, (iv) human interest?
4 Are there any columns devoted to (i) books, (ii) art, (iii) radio, (iv) television, (v) cinema?
5 Are the headlines an accurate summary of the news article or are they merely to attract readers?
6 Do you feel that any of the following qualities are present in the paper?

| Accuracy | Fair Play | Truthfulness |
| Responsibility | Independence | Sincerity |

7 Does the paper present news in an interesting manner?
8 Do you feel that the news is in any way distorted by emphasising certain items and suppressing others?
9 Who are the paper's competitors in the area?
10 What is the paper's outstanding feature?
11 Which of the following groups do you feel the paper is trying to attract?

| Teenagers | Working class | Middle class |
| Business people | House-wives | |

12 Has the paper a nickname? If so, why?
13 Has the paper an editorial policy?
14 Does this policy affect news articles?
15 Would you say that the paper is performing a community service? Does it participate in welfare and community projects such as the provision of playing-fields, community centre, etc.
16 Does the paper present value for money?

Use the information you have gathered to write an article of 500 words on the subject of your local paper.

98

Write a short story or a play and introduce the scenes depicted in the following six pictures. You may use the pictures in any order you wish.

99

The following graph summarises the financial and trading position of a company over ten years. Study the graph and then write about 150 words conveying the information you have gathered and the inferences drawn. Exact figures need not be quoted.

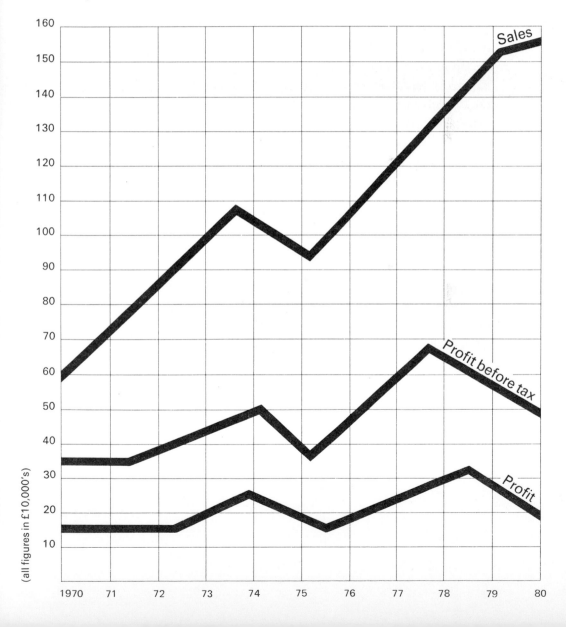

(all figures in £10,000's)

100

Read the following poem quickly in order to gain a general impression and then study it with care.

Marsh Marigolds

Where the brake is a tangle of dead stalks
and the black water stands in pools, the marsh
marigold lights the shadows. These flowers
are lamps that flame up steadily from green depths.
The green sepals unlock a tide of gold;
the stamens are rods and spikes of metal
in the polished flower cup. These flowers lie
couched upon themselves, petalless, but nested
upon their broadly heart-shaped leaves that grow
suddenly when the blossoms have opened,
as if to hold aloft their unclenched lights
that signal in dense river meadows and
wet copses. Sometimes a walker unsure
of the wood makes through the thickening growth
by the riverside, pushing dead ahead
in a quick racket of snapping dry sticks
and hissing leaves, and surprises these yellow
blooms promising water, in some dim place
whose stillness questions all his purposes.

GENE BARO

Write an appreciation of 'Marsh Marigolds'. Start with a brief summary and then go on to describe the form of the poem and its appeal. Give your views on its success or otherwise, whether or not you like it, and the reasons for your views.

Either (*a*) imagine you are the woman in the photograph and write an account of
what happened;

Or   (*b*) write the story which will accompany the photograph in the local newspaper.

Extract the main points of information from this photograph of a timber wharf at Tacoma, Washington, USA, and summarise them in good, continuous prose using not less than 150 words.

103

Summarise in not more than 200 words the ideas about failure that emerge from the following transcript of a radio interview.

Jocelyn Ryder-Smith I think most of us find failure is a very difficult thing to deal with in our lives. Why is it that we find it so very hard?

James Hemming Deep down we all have a profound sense of uncertainty about ourselves—a feeling of inadequacy. Failure confirms and reinforces this and, naturally, we find this painful. Also, as a species we are very status conscious, and failure produces loss of face, so we resist situations which seem likely to lead us towards failure.

Ryder-Smith You say everybody has a feeling of inadequacy somewhere deep inside them, but not everyone *seems* to feel this.

Hemming The appearance of immunity is to some extent a masquerade. We all feel inadequate at times because we all start weak and small in a big strong world, and first impressions go very deep. We never quite lose the feeling that the forces around us are too powerful for us.

Ryder-Smith Is it possible to learn to accept failure?

Hemming I think we must. Failure is part of success; in a way it's the springboard to success. Success is good for us, because it peps up our confidence, but it's our failures that teach us how we can adjust better to life and our friends. If we were never conscious of failure, we should never progress. We learn from our failures.

Ryder-Smith So what should we do when we're faced with a failure?

Hemming First of all we need to accept that, when something goes wrong, it can't just be somebody else's fault—it must be partly our fault. For instance, if a marriage breaks down, there's no point in saying, 'I'm no good', or 'All men are impossible', or 'Marriage can't work'. None of these things is true. But what is valuable is to ask, 'What made things go wrong? What was my contribution, and what were other people's contributions?' This way we can learn, and next time be in better shape to do rather better—not perfectly, but rather better. A lot of second marriages are very successful.

Ryder-Smith How important is it to be able to admit to other people that we were wrong?

Hemming Very important. This is the birth of maturity. While we are very young we seem to pick up this concept that we've got to be perfect all the time, but this is not true. There's no law of nature that says we've got to be perfect, or right, all the time. What we can do is to try to be as effective as possible in any particular situation. But we cannot always be wise; we do make mistakes; we do go wrong. The realisation that to be human is to be incomplete and imperfect is very important indeed. But we can all move from a minus to a plus in some fields of our lives. The great thing is to keep striving.

Ryder-Smith But if we have a sense of failure it's often terribly hard to keep on trying. A feeling of defeat just holds us back.

Hemming Here I think we must accept that day-dreams of quick success can never become reality—we cannot expect to succeed in one quick bound. The decision to change is the beginning of a process during which we shall often regress. We've got to keep our eye on the objective, and be prepared to fail and fail and fail again, and try and try and try again. That's how we progress in anything. I think a child in a free situation in the classroom is a good example of this: he'll try something and fail, and he will then go back to something he can do well, to reassure himself. He'll do it over and over again. Then he'll return to the thing he failed at and perhaps go a bit further this time, but fail again. Once more, he will go back to the activity where he can succeed, to rebuild his confidence, and then he will return to the difficult thing and so on until he has mastered it.

Ryder-Smith Sometimes failure at one thing gives us the feeling that we're total failures, failures as people. Is there any way of avoiding this?

Hemming There is no such thing as a person who is a failure. We can fail at any number of things but we must never identify ourselves with our failures. Rudyard Kipling once said that failure and success were both imposters, and I think that's quite true. Failure happens to us, but it isn't us.

104

The following table gives the results of a fifth year examination taken by candidates in the schools of a particular area. The results are in five grades and the table shows the number reaching each grade out of 100 candidates in each subject. It should be noted that a certain number of candidates in each subject failed to gain a grade.

Study the table carefully then state what conclusions you draw regarding (a) girls compared with boys as examination candidates, and (b) the implied advantages or disadvantages of single sex and co-educational schools.

Subject	Girls' Schools Grade				
	1	2	3	4	5
English	13	20	30	26	7
Mathematics	10	13	24	29	11
History	16	18	26	30	7
Geography	13	17	20	27	12
Biology	19	15	33	23	3
Physics	4	9	28	35	9
General Science	9	14	29	32	5

Subject	Boys' Schools Grade				
	1	2	3	4	5
English	9	16	23	32	10
Mathematics	16	11	23	24	14
History	11	16	31	31	5
Geography	9	10	26	37	9
Biology	4	8	29	35	13
Physics	20	14	29	23	5
General Science	17	21	25	27	8

Subject	Mixed Schools Grade				
	1	2	3	4	5
English	7	10	18	26	15
Mathematics	13	15	19	31	9
History	10	9	24	34	11
Geography	6	7	26	35	13
Biology	8	12	27	35	9
Physics	9	12	26	31	10
General Science	12	11	31	31	7

105

The pictures in this section are taken from a BBC television production of *War and Peace*. They show Russian prisoners being executed by a French firing squad for setting fire to houses in Moscow. The incident is but one of many that took place during Napoleon's occupation of Moscow in 1812. Look at the pictures carefully as they will help you to approach the writing that follows with interest and imagination.

1 Place yourself in the position of one of the French soldiers in the firing squad. Can your action be justified? How might you explain it to someone at a later date?
2 Imagine that you are one of the Russian prisoners. Tell the story of your capture, imprisonment and subsequent escape from the firing squad.
3 Write a piece of description, or a story, suggested to you by the pictures. You may use any method you like, e.g. diary, extract from a novel, short story, play, autobiography, etc.

The pictures you have studied express in visual terms for television the passage that follows.

From Prince Shcherbatov's house the prisoners were conducted straight down the Dyevichy meadow to the left of the nunnery as far as a kitchen-garden where a post had been set up. Beyond the post a big pit had been freshly dug in the ground, and a great crowd formed a semicircle about the post and the pit. The crowd consisted of a few Russians and a large proportion of soldiers from Napoleon's army not on duty—there were Germans, Italians and Frenchmen in a variety of uniforms. To right and left of the post stood rows of French soldiers in blue uniforms with red epaulets and high boots and shakos.

The prisoners were placed in a certain order, in accordance with a written list (Pierre was sixth), and led up to the post. A number of drums suddenly began beating on both sides of them, and Pierre felt that with the roll of drums part of his soul had been torn away. He lost all capacity to think and understand. He could only look and listen. And he had only one desire—the desire that the dreadful thing which had to be done should be done as quickly as possible. Pierre looked round at his companions and studied their faces.

The first two were convicts with shaven heads. One was tall and thin; the other a dark, shaggy, muscular fellow with a flat nose. No. 3 was a house-serf, a man of five-and-forty, with grizzled hair and a plump, well-nourished body. The fourth was a peasant, a very handsome fellow with a full flaxen beard and black eyes. The

fifth was a factory hand, a thin, sallow-faced lad of eighteen in a loose coat.

Pierre heard the French deliberating whether to shoot them singly or two at a time. 'In couples', the officer in command replied in a voice of cold indifference. There was a stir in the ranks of the soldiers and it was observable that they were all in a hurry—not as men hurry to execute an order they understand but as people make haste to have done with an essential but unpleasant and incomprehensible task.

A French official wearing a scarf came up to the right of the file of prisoners, and read out the sentence in Russian and French.

Then two pairs of French soldiers advanced to the criminals, and at the officer's command took the two convicts who stood first in the row. The convicts stopped when they reached the post and, while the sacks were being brought, looked dumbly about them, as a wounded animal watches the approaching huntsman. One of them kept crossing himself, the other scratched his back and worked his lips into the semblance of a smile. With hasty fingers the soldiers blindfolded them, drawing the sacks over their heads, and pinioned them to the post.

A dozen sharpshooters with muskets stepped out of the ranks with a firm, regular tread, and halted eight paces from the post. Pierre turned away so as not to see what was about to happen. There was a sudden rattle and crash which seemed to him louder than the most terrific thunderclap, and he looked round. There was some smoke, and the French soldiers, with pale faces and trembling hands, were doing something near the pit. Two more prisoners were led up. They, too, with the same silent appeal for protection in their eyes, gazed vainly round at the on-lookers, evidently unable to comprehend or believe what was coming. They were incredulous because they alone knew what their life meant to them, and so they could not understand, could not believe that it could be taken away from them.

The script of the television production covers the same scene in the following manner.

Telecine 1 :

Ext. A Meadow. Day

CLOSE TRACKING SHOT: PIERRE, walking in line with about
FIFTEEN OTHER RUSSIANS, most of them from the cell.

A drum beats a 'Left' beat to keep them in some sort of order.

LONG SHOT: THE COLUMN, being marched by FRENCH SOLDIERS over the meadow. Ahead of them, we can see a SMALL CROWD OF FRENCH SOLDIERS, not on duty, which has gathered to watch the scene. Standing to one side is a line of about a DOZEN SOLDIERS, very obviously on duty.

CLOSE ON: FRENCH CAPTAIN, shouting.

> *Captain:* Halt!

NEW ANGLE: The Line of PRISONERS, coming to a ragged halt. PIERRE is about seventh in line.

NEW SHOT: PIERRE, staring bewildered at the FRENCH SOLDIERS, not understanding still, what is going on.

HIS VIEWPOINT: A few yards in front of them, the FRENCH CAPTAIN is in consultation with another FRENCH OFFICER. Some yards behind them, two posts have been dug into the ground and behind them a pit has been dug, the earthwork piled to one side.

NEW ANGLE: PIERRE, staring at the scene. Just in front of him stands the BOY and a MAN wearing glasses.

> *Boy:* (BEWILDERED) What are they going to do? Are they going to—to...

He trails off, swallowing hard. The MAN doesn't reply. He stares white-faced at the posts and the pit behind. The BOY turns to PIERRE, his eyes wide.

> *Boy:* Sir—are they going to shoot us, sir?

PIERRE stares at him but doesn't answer. He looks incredulously about him, still not prepared to grasp the meaning of what is about to happen.

NEW SHOT: THE FRENCH OFFICER in consultation with the CAPTAIN breaks off and marches over to the line of FRENCH SOLDIERS. We hear commands in French ring out. The FIRST TWO SOLDIERS detach themselves from the rank and march towards the RUSSIAN PRISONERS.

At the same time, the rest of the SOLDIERS, about TEN
OF THEM, march smartly in line towards the posts,
wheel and line up facing them about ten paces distant.
CLOSE SHOT: THE FIRST TWO PRISONERS. THE TWO
SOLDIERS halt beside them, turn about to face in the
same direction, taken each an arm and march forward.
THE TWO RUSSIANS look bewildered, as if not realizing
what is about to happen to them. THE FRENCH
SOLDIERS keep their eyes averted. CLOSE GROUP SHOT:
MAN with glasses, the BOY and PIERRE.

> *Boy*: But what are they going to do? (TO PIERRE)
> Mister, what are they going to? (cont...)

No one speaks. Every eye is trained unbelievingly on
the drama they know is about to unfold. The BOY lets
out a quiet sob.

> *Boy*: (cont) I want to go home—I want to go home—

NEW SHOT: THE POSTS, with the TWO PRISONERS standing in front of them, their arms being tied to the
posts. They look dumbly about them as the ritual
proceeds.
THEIR VIEWPOINT: THE FIRING SQUAD, waiting
impassively.
CLOSE SHOT: TWO DRUMMERS, drumsticks poised,
waiting the order to roll.
NEW ANGLE: THE TWO PRISONERS, standing with sacks
37 over their heads, now completely anonymous. The
TWO SOLDIERS who brought them are marching back
across the meadow towards the PRISONERS to get the
next two.

> *Captain*: (IN FRENCH) Ready!

CLOSE SHOT: THE DRUMMERS, rolling the drums in a
long, frightening roll.

> *Captain*: (O.S.) Aim! (cont...)

BOU PIERRE, suddenly closing his eyes as he waits the
final command. The drums continue rolling.

NEW SHOT: THE FIRING SQUAD, rifles aimed, waiting. The
VICTIMS tied to the posts; the FRENCH CAPTAIN.

> *Captain:* (cont) Fire!

There is volley of shots and the TWO BODIES on the
posts sag against the ropes. The drums cease.

CLOSE GROUP SHOT: THE MAN with the glasses and
THE BOY and PIERRE. The next two PRISONERS are
already being marched off out of shot.

> *Boy:* (WHIMPERING) I didn't do nothing, I didn't,
> I didn't ...

PIERRE doesn't reply. He stares, white-faced at the
scene in front of him.

NEW SHOT: THE BODIES of the TWO EXECUTED VICTIMS
are being placed in the pit. At the same time, the next
TWO are being stood in front of the posts and tied to
them.

Make a close study of the pictures, the extract from the novel, and the television script and then answer the questions that follow.

1 Write out the shots in the script that are illustrated by the first three pictures.

2 Study the pictures again. What do you think of the setting and the costumes? Are they a faithful interpretation of the extract from the novel?

3 Do the pictures and the script spoil the extract for you or do they make it more interesting and enjoyable? Explain why this is so.

4 In the extract from the novel the 'sallow-faced lad of eighteen' has nothing to say. In the script he is called THE BOY and has five lines to speak. What is the effect on the scene of the inclusion of these five lines?

5 Study the tone and feeling of the lines for THE BOY. How do they indicate his emotional attitude?

6 In what ways do PIERRE and THE BOY differ in this scene?

7 Give reasons why you do or do not think that the script is largely in keeping with the extract.

8 The word TELECINE at the beginning of the script indicates that the scene is to be filmed and then inserted into the studio action Why do you think it was necessary to shoot this scene on film?

9 In television drama the expression on the face of a character is often used to replace a line of dialogue. Give two examples from the script where PIERRE might have replied to THE BOY but a camera shot was used instead.

10 At a number of places in the script the cameraman is asked to use close shots. Suggest other places where you consider a close shot would be effective.

11 Imagine that you are involved in the design side of a television production of a 19th century Russian novel. Use school and public libraries to do background research on costumes, furniture, buildings and music of the period. Present the results of your research in the form of notes accompanied by sketches of (a) costumes for one male and one female character, and (b) a house interior or some pieces of furniture to be used. Supplement this with an account of the music to be played or a taped recording.

12 Should experiences of this nature be shown on television? Refer in your discussion to this scene and also to anything similar you have seen on television.

13 Study the pictures, the extract and the script and then make an interesting review of the scene for a popular newspaper.

14 Imagine you are PIERRE. Describe your thoughts and feelings as you live through this experience.
15 Write a scene for television on a theme of your own choosing. Give your script the same layout as for the excerpt on p. 210.
16 Summarise the extract from the novel in 100 words for someone who has not read it.
17 Nineteenth century Russian fiction is one of the richest periods of any literature in the world. Two well-known authors of that time were Nikolay Gogol and Anton Chekhov. Choose one of these for detailed study. Find out what you can about his background and the books he wrote. If possible read one of his short stories, e.g. *The Overcoat* by Gogol or *The Lady with the Dog* by Chekhov. Use your research to write an informative article about the writer.

G.K

Reference Section

Expression of Organised Thoughts in Writing

1 Gather your material

(a) Do all your reading first and make notes as you go along.

(b) Jot down ideas as they pass through your mind.

(c) Obtain other people's opinions on the subject.

2 Plan on paper before writing

(a) Limit your topic—don't try to solve the world's problems on one sheet of paper.

(b) Express in one sentence what you hope to accomplish and this will give you your theme.

(c) Select a starting-point and an ending.

(d) Arrange your notes and ideas; go straight from the starting point to the end.

(e) Take out anything which has no bearing on the subject.

(f) Set out paragraph headings.

3 Write with the plan before you

(a) Be precise with words, never be content with a word which does not fit your need.

(b) Use concrete and colourful words.

(c) Use a dictionary and a thesaurus.

(d) Look ahead and consider words and phrases.

(e) Make your opening and concluding sentences carefully worded, exact and interesting.

(f) Vary short and long sentences.

(g) Make every sentence follow naturally from the previous one.

(h) Think about grammar and punctuation.

(i) Confine one topic to one paragraph.

(j) Make clear early in the paragraph what the topic is.

(k) Follow the rules of writing you have been taught.

43 Apsley Street,
Windsor,
Berkshire.

YOUR ADDRESS

REFERENCE

Ref: AMS/pb

THEIR ADDRESS

Mr. John Roberts,
24 Parkside Drive,
Reading,
Berkshire.

13th September

DATE

SALUTATION

Dear Sir,

BODY

    This business letter has eight standard parts. The recipient's address is generally omitted from a personal letter. If the letter to which you are replying has a reference on it, then this should be quoted.

    The body of the letter is the most important part and it may have one paragraph or several. Paragraphs deal with one point at a time and are indented.

Yours faithfully,

SUBSCRIPTION

J B Howard

J.B. Howard
Advertising Manager

SIGNATURE

Writing a Summary

There are many everyday activities that involve making a summary even though this name may not be used. A description to a friend of a book, a film, or a television programme is a summary of what you have experienced. Local, national and world events are summarised for the newspapers and also for the news on radio and television. The synopsis of a play, the film notes in the local paper, the telegram you send instead of a letter are all summaries; so are the abstracts used by doctors and scientists and the brief used by the lawyer.

To write an effective summary you must be able to grasp the line of thought and the main ideas in a piece of writing, and then re-express these in language of your own, in a smaller number of words than the original. Summarisation is therefore a test of reading and writing, for you cannot make a summary of a passage unless you understand it and can convey that understanding in your own words. The essentials for a summary therefore, are as follows:

(i) an understanding of what is read;
(ii) the discrimination and judgement needed to select from it what is important;
(iii) the expression of this in direct and economical English using your own words and sentence construction.

It will be seen that more is needed than the simple cutting down of the number of words in the original. Some students, when faced with the task of cutting a passage to one-third of its length, have been known to take out every third sentence, or cross out words and phrases here and there, and then write out the remainder. This is not a summary because the aim of summarisation is not to select a third of the ideas and major points; the aim is to get as many of them as you can, and this always involves rewriting the passage.

A good plan for making a summary is as follows:

1 Read and reread the passage until you have understood it. If the passage is a difficult one it may be necessary to read it at least four times before you grasp the line of thought and pick out the main points.

2 Try to sum up the passage in a sentence or two and then condense this to make a title. Study the paragraph divisions as they may give you three or four subtitles. Take a sheet of paper and list the essential points of the passage under the title and the subtitles. Where possible replace a phrase by a single word; do not bother with repetitions, examples and illustrations. There is no need to replace each essential word by a synonym or paraphrase all important phrases,

but use your own words as far as possible. You are more likely to do this if you can work without the original.

3 Check with the original to make sure that all the essential (and none of the trivial) points have been included.

4 Put the original aside and on another sheet of paper write out the points you have selected in clear, continuous English. Paragraphing is not required for a summary. If the passage contains words actually spoken then your summary must be in indirect speech because the words are no longer the words of the speaker. Introduce them by writing, 'The — said that . . . ', and put the remainder in the past tense.

5 It is usual to either shorten a passage by one-third or work to a maximum number of words, so check your rough draft. If it is too long then make economies by saving words here and there without sacrificing the meaning or the style. If it is too short it would be wise to study the original to see if anything of importance has been left out. Make any other alterations you feel are necessary and then compare it with the original to see if it is an adequate summary. It is a good idea to view your summary from the standpoint of the person who is going to read it, and ask yourself if it contains the points necessary to give that reader all that is important and essential.

6 Copy the summary out neatly and remember that whoever reads it will also be influenced by clear writing and a good layout.

Much practice is needed to become an efficient summariser but it is worth persevering with because you will develop your powers of judgement, concentration and expression, and these qualities will stand you in good stead throughout your life.

How to Make Notes

Note-making is an essential skill for anyone wanting to make progress at school, at college, or at work. The higher you go as a student, the greater the need to take notes. If you are ambitious it will not be long before you are called upon to make a speech or take part in a discussion; notes made beforehand will help you to keep to the point and include all the ideas you wish to put across. Trades and professions do not stand still and there is a constant stream of new ideas and techniques appearing in books, trade journals and newspapers. Note-making will enable you to select what you want from this mass of information and thereby keep up to date.

Notes are made in order to store essential information in a space-saving form for use at a later date. If the aim is to use them for revision, then they must help recall the most important points of information in order to save the time and trouble of referring again to the original. They can be taken from the spoken word, the printed word, or from visual material.

Notes made of a speech or a lecture are more difficult to make than any other and their success will depend upon the ability of the speaker. A good speaker or lecturer will have an Introduction, followed by an Explanation, a Repetition of the main points, and a Summary with which to close. Unfortunately, many speakers will wander off the point and not stick to this outline. It will be necessary to listen carefully, especially for such phrases as

'We now turn to . . .'

'There are several ways of . . .'

'I am going to deal with . . .'

for these usually introduce information to be noted. Use a proper notebook at lectures, number your notes, and don't use abbreviations that you will not be able to understand later on. It is worth remembering that notes taken at a lecture may be the only method of revision or reference at a later date. Skill in note-making from speeches can be developed by making use of BBC programmes. Select a talk in which you are interested and try to make notes as you listen. An alternative method of practise is to arrange with your teacher for a student to prepare and deliver a short speech while the remainder of the class make notes. With this method it is possible for you to compare the notes you have made with the original plan or notes for the lecture.

Notes made from the printed word must be done with care and accuracy and follow an orderly arrangement. If they are not made to a definite plan, which is a skeleton of the original, then the eye cannot easily take them in at first glance when they are needed. This would represent time wasted in making the notes, for it would be just as easy to read the original.

The essentials in a plan for note-making are a Title, Headings for the main points and Subheadings for the rest of the information. It is also useful to link roman numerals with Headings, capital letters with subheadings, and arabic numerals and small letters for subdividing the remainder of the information. The method is best illustrated by making notes from an actual passage and pointing out the steps to be taken.

Read through the following passage and make sure you understand it.

Flint is a rock which consists of silica in non-crystalline form—the crystalline form being quartz. The silica from which flint has been derived was originally the skeletons of sponges. These dissolved, and the silica was re-deposited in bands of flint. Flint may be found in regular layers in chalk. When the irregular grey lumps are broken into small fragments, they usually disclose, somewhere in the middle, a fossil sponge, round which the silica was deposited gradually. The flint layers, therefore, probably represent beds in which fossil sponges were particularly abundant on the sea floor.

Flint has been of considerable importance in human history. Because it breaks into flakes and fragments with very sharp edges, it was used for the making of knives, spearheads, and many other tools and weapons in the early days of mankind. Flint was also used for making fire, and until recently houses were often built of flints set in mortar. Today flints are heated in kilns to provide soft white silica powder for the manufacture of white porcelain tiles.

When exposed to the weather, flint develops a white matt surface by the dissolving of the silica from the exterior layers. The thickness of this white layer gives some idea of the length of time the flint has been exposed to the weather, and from this some idea can be obtained of the age of flint implements. Flints were used from the days of prehistoric man to historic times.

Oxford Junior Encyclopaedia, Vol. III, p. 166

To make notes on this passage a process of investigation and analysis is followed.

1 A title is needed. What is the passage about? FLINT. This is printed in capital letters against the left-hand margin and underlined. At the same level, but on

the right-hand side, a note is made of the source in case it is required at a later date.

2 The headings are the next step. What are the paragraphs about? Does the topic or key sentence give a heading or a clue? A further study of the three paragraphs shows that they deal with,

(i)   a description of flint and its origin;

(ii) its use by man;

(iii) the weathering of flint.

These three summaries will provide the headings required, if the word 'flint' which is in the title is dropped, and inessential words are left out.

3 Take the first heading, DESCRIPTION AND ORIGIN, give it a roman numeral, print it against the left-hand margin and below the title, and then underline it.

4 Subheadings are now required for this first heading. An examination of the first paragraph shows that flint is defined as a rock and it originated from the sea floor. The subheadings can therefore be (i) Rock, and (ii) Origin. Never use a single Subheading: always use at least two.

5 Give this subheading a capital letter, indent under the first heading and underline.

6 Further information is now extracted from the first paragraph and put down in words and phrases under Rock. Each new point begins with an arabic numeral and a capital letter on a new line, and all the lines are immediately below each other. Information relating to each point can be given a small letter and inset again. Important phrases can be lifted from the original as this is accepted in note-making.

7 The Subheading, Origin, is dealt with in the same way and the notes now look like this.

FLINT   from *Oxford Junior Encyclopaedia*, Vol. III, p. 166

I DESCRIPTION AND ORIGIN

  A ROCK
    1 Non-crystalline form of silica
    2 Grey colour, irregular shape
    3 Found in chalk

B ORIGIN
  1 Sea floor
  2 Sponge skeleton
  - (*a*) dissolved and re-deposited
  - (*b*) fossil sponge inside rock
  3 Layers were sponge beds

8 The procedure outlined in 3, 4, 5, and 6 is now repeated for the second heading —USE BY MAN, and the third heading—WEATHERING.

9 Complete the notes for this passage to make sure that you have grasped the procedure involved, and then compare your notes with the final set given below. There will probably be some slight differences but the main points should be the same.

FLINT
from *Oxford Junior Encyclopaedia*, Vol. III, p. 166

I DESCRIPTION AND ORIGIN

A ROCK
  1 Non-crystalline form of silica
  2 Grey colour, irregular shape
  3 Found in chalk

B ORIGIN
  1 Sea floor
  2 Sponge skeleton
  - (*a*) dissolved and re-deposited
  - (*b*) fossil sponge inside rock
  3 Layers were sponge beds

II USE BY MAN

A PREHISTORIC
  1 Tools and weapons
  - (*a*) flakes easily, sharp edges
  2 Making fire
B RECENT: Building houses—set in mortar
C CURRENT: White porcelain tiles—silica powder by kiln heating

III WEATHERING

A EXTERIOR

   1 White matt surface develops
   2 Surface thickness denotes age

It can now be seen why headings are underlined and subheadings are underlined and inset. The visual pattern of the notes is quickly taken in by the eye and the main features and the details are easily assimilated. The original needed careful searching for the information now laid out so clearly.

Notes taken from visual material will follow the same plan as that given for the printed word. A title is found which sums up the whole, and the headings and subheadings correspond to areas of the picture, or sections of the diagram, from which information is extracted.

The layout of notes for a speech is not so detailed because the notes are for personal use and they are not permanent. Normally they consist of words and phrases to remind the speaker of what comes next.

Note-making offers an important training in judgement and in the art of selecting important facts and ideas. It has been considered here in some detail because it is an essential skill which in the past has been neglected.

The Interpretation of Statistics

The three main methods of presenting information are by language, by figures, and by pictures, and each of these methods has its own peculiar advantages. Language is the most expressive and adaptable, figures are a shorthand for representing actual quantities and the relationships between them, and pictures are useful for indicating shapes, forms, and the layout of things. Sometimes the three methods overlap and the information given in one form can be re-expressed in another; it is with this re-expression that we are concerned here.

The presentation of information in figures (statistics) is common to many trades and professions and is also popular in newspapers, magazines and books, and on television and film. When considering statistics in any media it is wise to check the source, the accuracy they can be expected to have, and how much is being read into them. Figures can give a misleading impression, whether this is by intention or otherwise.

The interpretation of statistical data has become a skill important enough for some examining boards to set questions asking the candidate to write a short article on the facts disclosed by a group of figures. What is required in this type of question is a reproduction of the information conveyed by the general trend of the figures, the drawing of attention to any significant variations from this trend, and a suggested explanation of the disclosed facts. The article should never be a mere representation of figures in word form and the interpretation should be made as interesting as possible. The three essentials in an exercise of this nature are:

1 common sense and imagination to dig out the facts;
2 some general knowledge in order to give an explanation;
3 skill in the writing of an article.

As an example let us take a simple case of figures relating to street accidents in the imaginary town of Portsea.

Street Accidents

	AGE 7–15	AGE 15–60	OVER 60
TIME			
Before 9 am	41	25	21
9 am to 12 noon	14	32	28
12 noon to 2 pm	49	36	17
2 pm to 4 pm	24	26	42
4 pm to 7 pm	53	42	16
After 7 pm	24	84	13

Examine the figures very carefully, make a note of any general trend, and give some thought to the reason for it. If there is no general trend then this fact should also be noted. Any variations or exceptions disclosed should be jotted down and an attempt made to find the cause. Speculations about such causes should always be close to the facts, reasonable, and within the bounds of probability. The facts and the inferences to be drawn from them are then noted down as follows:

1 Accidents are heaviest amongst schoolchildren after school is over. *Inference:* Some alternative needed to playing on the streets.

2 Accidents among schoolchildren are also heavy when they are going to or returning from school. *Inference:* Drivers should be more careful during these hours, especially near schools.

3 The greatest number of accidents occur after 7 pm and especially in the 15–60 age group. *Inference:* As these are fairly responsible people it would seem that the roads are not so safe in the evening as they are in the day. Further figures for winter and summer accidents would help towards a more definite conclusion.

4 Accidents amongst those over 60 are heaviest between 2 pm and 4 pm. *Inference:* This is to be expected since these are the hours when most elderly people go walking.

5 The general conclusion is that accidents are far too numerous and some suggestions as to how they could be reduced might be included.

As a rule the facts can be arranged chronologically, but if not they should be dealt with group by group. The notes should then be written up in simple, straightforward English.

The presentation of numerical facts in diagrams, graphs and pictures has become increasingly popular in the mass media because this method gives a more vivid impression of the main points, and their significance is grasped more easily than with the equivalent table of figures or lengthy description. The interpretation of diagrams, graphs and pictures is therefore easier so far as the significant facts are concerned. The procedure to be followed is the same as that used for the interpretation of statistics and may be summed up as follows:

1 make notes on the main facts;

2 note any inferences which may be drawn;

3 use a logical arrangement and write the article from the notes.

There are other kinds of information that can be presented only in a certain pictorial manner, such as maps and plans, and examples are given in this book to enable you to practise the skill required to translate the information gained into words.

Comprehension

The main purpose of setting a passage for comprehension is to improve your power of understanding by asking questions designed to make you look more closely at what you read. In addition, the passage may help you to refine your vocabulary by seeing words correctly used, and also help to develop your awareness of language and your powers of analysis and criticism.

The passages in this book come not only from the writer who wishes to communicate an experience which he believes is worthy of consideration, but also from the man who has been trained to use words effectively in order to sell you some ideas you might not otherwise have had or wanted. The work of the writer who slants the news, or who persuades in the advertisement, needs as close a study as that of the serious writer.

Your own written work will lead you to realise that any piece of writing is an example of the way a particular writer assembles facts and opinions in language suited to his purpose. It is wise, therefore, to make sure that you are aware of the author's attitude to his subject in any passage you study. Does he present information or ideas uncoloured by his own feelings as in the extract on page 160? Does he, like the writer on page 109, select his material and then persuade you by use of language to adopt his selection? Will you have to clarify in your own mind, by a study of the words used, an attitude which is not openly stated as in the assignment on page 60?

Once the author's attitude to his subject is established, the best way to tackle a passage for comprehension is to read it through once or twice, and then read it again with the question in mind so as to decide which part or parts of the passage answer the question. Some of the more common forms of question will require you to give:

(i)   meanings of words and phrases as used in the passage;
(ii) explanations in your own words of expressions used;
(iii) reactions to the passage in terms of emotion felt, attitude to contents, and feelings of approval and disapproval;
(iv) summaries of parts or aspects of the passage.

Apart from these you should always ensure that you have mastered the meanings of words and phrases if they are new to you. It is also a good exercise to reproduce in your own words the important points from what you have read, as this is a test of understanding and not just memorisation.

It is hoped that some of the passages set for comprehension will tempt you to read the book from which they were taken, and with that end in view, a source list is given on page 232.

Further Reading

1 Source List

ANOUILH, JEAN *Becket* Samuel French

BETTI, UGO 'Summertime', from *Three Plays* Gollancz

COTTRELL, LEONARD *The Roman Forts of the Saxon Shore* HMSO

DRINKWATER, JOHN *Abraham Lincoln* Samuel French

FROST, ROBERT *Penguin Poets: Robert Frost* Penguin

JOHNSON, T. E. *One Off—The Story of an Advertising Man* Educational Explorers

JOYCE, JAMES *Portrait of the Artist as a Young Man* Penguin

KESSEL, N., and WALTON, H. *Alcoholism* Penguin

OMMANNEY, F. D. *Eastern Windows* Longman

Parents, Children and Television HMSO

RATTIGAN, TERENCE *Ross (A Dramatic Portrait)* Hamish Hamilton

SILVER, P. S. *Venereal Disease* Bolton Civic Centre

SMITH, EMMA *Maidens' Trip* Penguin

TOLSTOY, LEO *War and Peace* Penguin

WAUGH, EVELYN *Scoop* Longman (HLS)

WILLIAMS, TENNESSEE *The Night of the Iguana* Penguin

WOOLLEY, SIR LEONARD *History Unearthed* Benn

2 Social Problems

BALDWIN, JAMES *The Fire Next Time* Penguin

FINCH, BERNARD *Passport to Paradise* Arco

GRIFFIN, JOHN HOWARD *Black Like Me* Panther

MACKEY, H. O. *A Handbook on Alcoholism* Macmillan

MCINNES, COLIN *City of Spades* Penguin

RICHMOND, A. H. *Colour Problem* Penguin

RUSSELL, BERTRAND *Unarmed Victory* Penguin

SAGAN, FRANÇOISE *Toxique* Souvenir Press

SCHUR, EDWIN *Narcotic Addiction in Britain and America* Tavistock Pub.

VD: The Facts BMA (Family Doctor Booklet)

WEATHERBY, W. J. *Breaking the Silence* Penguin

WYKES, ALAN *The Doctor and His Enemy* Joseph

3 Relationships

BARSTOW, STAN *A Kind Loving* Penguin

BOWEN, ELIZABETH *The Death of the Heart* Penguin

DRABBLE, MARGARET *The Millstone* Longman Imprint Books

GREENE, GRAHAM *Brighton Rock* Penguin

MCCULLERS, CARSON *Member of the Wedding* Penguin

SALINGER, J. D. *Catcher in the Rye* Penguin

LAWRENCE, D. H. *The Rainbow* Penguin

4 The Mass Media

(a) General

HALL, S., and WHANNEL, P. *The Popular Arts* Hutchinson

THOMPSON, DENYS (Ed.) *Discrimination and Popular Culture* Penguin

HOGGART, RICHARD *The Uses of Literacy* Penguin

MCLUHAN, MARSHALL *The Mechanical Bride* Routledge & Kegan Paul

WILLIAMS, RAYMOND *Communications* Penguin

(b) Advertising

BIRCH, LIONEL *The Advertising We Deserve?* Vista

HARRIS, R. and SELDON, A. *Advertising in Action* Hutchinson

MAYER, MARTIN *Madison Avenne* Penguin

PACKARD, VANCE *The Hidden Persuaders* Penguin

THOMPSON, DENYS *Voice of Civilisation* Muller

TURNER, E. S. *The Shocking History of Advertising* Penguin

(c) The Press

HMSO *The British Press*

BOSTON, RICHARD (Ed.) *The Press We Deserve* Routledge and Kegan Paul

MATTHEWS, T.S. *The Sugar Pill* Gollancz

THOMPSON, DENYS *Between the Lines* Muller

WILLIAMS, FRANCIS *Dangerous Estate* Longman

PEP *Performance of the Press*

(d) Television

HMSO *Sound and Television Broadcasting in Britain*

HIGGINS, A. P. *Talking about Television* British Film Institute

BAKEWELL, JOAN and GARNHAM, NICHOLAS *The New Priesthood* Penguin Press
HIMMELWEIT, H., OPPENHEIM, A., VINCE, P. *Television and the Child* OUP
TAYLOR, J. R. *Anatomy of a Television Play* Weidenfeld and Nicolson